# Learning to Learn English

## A course in learner training

## Teacher's Book

*Gail Ellis and
Barbara Sinclair*

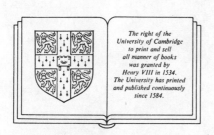

The right of the
University of Cambridge
to print and sell
all manner of books
was granted by
Henry VIII in 1534.
The University has printed
and published continuously
since 1584.

Cambridge University Press
Cambridge
New York   Port Chester
Melbourne   Sydney

*To Norman Whitney with thanks*

Published by the Press Syndicate of the University of Cambridge
The Pitt Building, Trumpington Street, Cambridge CB2 1RP
40 West 20th Street, New York, NY 10011–4211, USA
10 Stamford Road, Oakleigh, Victoria 3166, Australia

© Cambridge University Press 1989

First published 1989
Third printing 1991

Printed in Great Britain by Bell & Bain Ltd, Glasgow

ISBN 0 521 33817 4   Teacher's Book
ISBN 0 521 33816 6   Learner's Book
ISBN 0 521 32876 4   Cassette

# Contents

# Acknowledgements

We would like to thank the following people for their patience, support and encouragement: the Ellis family, Philip W. Sinclair, David Wharry and Helen Woodeson.

We are also grateful to the following:
Colleagues and pupils in France and at the British Council, Paris, 1983–7; colleagues and learners at the British Council, Munich, 1983–7 for providing valuable feedback; Peter Donovan and our editors Alison Baxter and Angela Wilde at Cambridge University Press for their interest, support and constructive advice; Roland Hindmarsh for providing the initial motivation; all those who gave us permission to record them and to use their photographs, examples of handwriting and points of view about language learning, and particularly Kate Pearce for her help; in addition, our thanks for all the guidance received from other sources.

We would like to thank the following people and institutions for piloting learner training materials and providing us with valuable feedback: Institut für Sprachwissenschaft, Universität Bern, Switzerland; The Bell School, Cambridge; Eurocentre, Cambridge; The Newnham Language Centre, Cambridge; Ecole des Cadres, Courbevoie, France; Infop, Dijon-Longvic, France; Exeter College, Exeter; Institute for English Language, University of Lancaster; Instituto de Idiomas, Lima, Peru; International House, London; Formation Continue, Université Lumière Lyon 2, Lyon, France; British Council, Madrid; AMES, Melbourne, Australia; RMIT, Melbourne, Australia; Godmer House, Oxford; Formatique Développement, Paris, France; Institut Universitaire de Technologie, Paris, France; Institut Catholique de Paris, Paris, France; AMES, Perth, Australia; FAO, Rome, Italy; Cambridge Centre for Languages, Sawston; Centre de Formation de Formateurs, Université des Sciences Humaines, Strasbourg, France; Stanton School of English, Tokyo, Japan; CAVILAM, Vichy, France; ENAC, Toulouse, France; Dr Anna Chamot; Liz Hamp-Lyons; Dr Michael O'Malley; Lorna Rowsell; Joan Rubin; Stephen Slater.

The authors and publishers are grateful to the following for permission to reproduce copyright material:
Michael Lewis (extracts from *The English Verb* on pp. 89, 90); Routledge & Kegan Paul Limited (extract from *The Languages of the World* on pp. 110, 111); Praetorius Limited (extract from *Language Monthly* on p. 110).

# Introduction

*Learning to Learn English* is a course of learner training for learners of English as a foreign or second language from lower-intermediate level upwards. It has the following aims:

1. To help learners consider the factors that affect their learning and discover the learning strategies that suit them best so that they may:
   – become more effective language learners
   – take on more responsibility for their own learning.

2. To provide language teachers with:
   – a framework for planning a course of learner training
   – a set of learner training materials and guidelines for their use in the classroom.

3. To help teachers use such a course of learner training together with their own language teaching syllabus and materials.

*Learning to Learn English* is based on recent research findings about second language acquisition and learning strategies and on practical experience of learner training in the classroom. The materials consist of:

*Learner's Book*: this contains a series of discussion points, activities and suggestions for more effective learning, as well as points of view about language learning and learning strategies from learners around the world. It is for use mainly in the classroom under the guidance of a teacher.

*Teacher's Book*: this contains an introduction to the theory of learner training, as well as detailed notes on how to implement the activities in the Learner's Book and integrate these into a language course. It also contains guidelines for adapting the activities to different teaching situations.

*Cassette*: this has recordings of native and non-native speakers of English which relate to the activities in the book.

# 1 The theory of learner training

> If you give a man a fish, you feed him for a day.
> If you teach a man to fish, you feed him for a lifetime.
>
> Confucius (551–479BC)

## The aims of learner training

Learner training aims to help learners consider the factors that affect their learning and discover the learning strategies that suit them best so that they may:

— become more effective learners
— take on more responsibility for their own learning.

It focusses their attention on the process of learning so that the emphasis is on *how* to learn rather than on *what* to learn.

Learner training is based on the following assumptions:
— that individuals learn in different ways and may use a variety of learning strategies at different times depending on a range of variables, such as the nature of the learning task, mood, motivation levels;
— that the more informed learners are about language and language learning the more effective they will be at managing their own learning.

Helping learners take on more responsibility for their own learning can be beneficial for the following reasons:
— learning can be more effective when learners take control of their own learning because they learn what they are ready to learn;
— those learners who are responsible for their own learning can carry on learning outside the classroom;
— learners who know about learning can transfer learning strategies to other subjects (adapted from Hallgarten and Rostworowska 1985:4).
Learner training, therefore, aims to provide learners with the alternatives from which to make informed choices about what, how, why, when and where they learn. This is not to say that they *have* to make all of these decisions all of the time. They may, indeed, choose to be teacher-dependent.

In order to be able to make such choices about their learning, it follows that the learners need to be informed about the language itself (through language awareness activities), about language learning techniques and processes (through experimentation and reflection) and about themselves as language learners (through regular self-assessment and introspection). We may hypothesise that as learners become more informed, so they will be in a better position to make these decisions. They are then also more likely to be more effective and better motivated as learners.

Learner training is, then, related to the concept of learner autonomy in that it aims to provide learners with the *ability*, that is strategies and confidence, to take on more responsibility for their own learning, although it does not thrust autonomy upon them. Instead, its aim is to *prepare* learners for independence. It recognises that the state of complete autonomy is an ideal rarely attained in any sphere of life, since people live in societies where they are affected by and affect others. It recognises, too, that some people prefer not to be independent at all times in their learning. Nevertheless, learner training espouses the belief that everybody has the right to develop the capacity for taking charge of his or her own affairs and that this development is a basic function of education.

The idea of learner training is not new, but there has recently been a revival of interest in this dimension of language teaching and learning. For example, in connection with the Council of Europe's Modern Languages Project, Holec (1981:23) wrote: 'Teaching must also help the learner acquire autonomy for himself, i.e. to learn to learn'. The revival is probably due to:
— the development of more learner-centred approaches, which have led to a greater focus on the learner as an individual and on the promotion of learner autonomy;
— the growth of a respect for the individual in society, in which the concept of autonomy is defined as the 'ability to assume responsibility for one's own affairs'*, and the opportunity to acquire this autonomy is viewed as a fundamental human right. This grew from the ideas of people such as Freire (1972), Illich (1973) and Rogers (1969) and has also led to a greater concern for the learners' linguistic and pedagogical rights (Gomes de Matos 1986).
As a result, many teachers have felt the need to expand their role (Wenden 1985b) by including, for example, language awareness activities, study skills, opportunities for learner choice and, more recently, by helping learners learn how to learn. The procedures and techniques for doing this have become known as learner training.

## Learner training or learner development?

More recently the term *learner development* has been suggested for what we have described as *learner training*, leaving learner training more narrowly defined as the promotion of the characteristics and behaviour of the 'good language learner', as identified by recent research (Rubin 1975, Stern 1975 and Naiman et al. 1978 – see page 5). In our view,

---

* Schwartz, B. 1977. *L'Education demain*. Aubier Montaigne, Paris. Quoted in Holec (1981:3).

this definition represents a superficial interpretation of some very useful and influential studies and we would agree with Wenden (1985b:989) when she says, 'The term [learner training] should not be understood in a narrow sense as the rote teaching of discrete behaviours.'

The term 'training' may seem to imply that learners are indeed taught specific behaviours rather than being encouraged to discover what works best for them as individuals. We use this term, however, because it is widely used and recognised by our profession; we do not intend it to be understood as in any sense referring to a prescriptive approach.

## Learner training and study skills

In recent years there has also been a growing interest in the area of study skills. Study skills for EFL and ESL, or English for Academic Purposes (EAP) as this area is sometimes known, equip learners with the skills required in order to succeed in a particular study environment, which has its own set of conventions. For example, a course which prepares foreign students for study at a British university requires students to be proficient in such skills as taking notes, preparing for seminars, organising and presenting essays (Wallace 1980). Other examples of study skills might be learning how to use a particular dictionary or the school library.

It is often claimed that the aims of study skills are very similar to those of learner training – and there is indeed an overlap (see Fig. 1). Our view is that study skills form a part of learner training and that learner training is more far-reaching, for the following reasons:

1. In study skills objectives are usually imposed from some external source, such as a set syllabus, specific assessment procedures or a particular cultural setting (although learners may indeed have the freedom to choose *how* to achieve these objectives). Learner training provides learners with more opportunity to select their own learning objectives.
2. Study skills tend to focus on the particular *products* required by a specific study context, such as passing examinations or writing a good précis. Learner training focusses on the *process* of learning in order to provide learners with wider insights into their own learning.
3. Study skills tend to involve learners in specific tasks or activities directly related to the requirements of their course of study. Learner training tends to provide more opportunities for learners to reflect on their attitudes towards themselves as learners and their personal learning preferences, as well as to experiment with different learning and practice activities in general.
4. Study skills usually prepare learners for an external system of assessment. Learner training trains them in self-assessment.

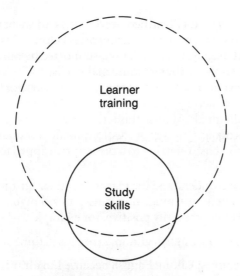

*Figure 1*

## Learner training and the 'good language learner'

Despite the current interest in learner training and the acceptance of its value, it still remains a secondary concern in many foreign language classrooms. This may be partly due to the fact that 'our knowledge about language learning is still very incomplete' (Stern 1983:410) and partly because there are relatively few learner training materials and guidelines for teachers on the market.

Carroll suggested (1967:104) that biographies of individuals speaking more than one language might contain clues to the conditions of successful language acquisition. From this suggestion came the idea of studying good language learners. A number of studies were carried out (Rubin 1975, Stern 1975, Naiman et al. 1978 among others). These studies produced inventories of the characteristics and learning strategies of good language learners which, although cautious about the findings, provided some useful insights into the foreign language learning process.

Perhaps the most significant finding with regard to learner training is the fact that these studies highlighted 'the complex interplay of factors potentially affecting success in language learning' (Fröhlich and Paribakht 1984:71); the 'uniqueness and individuality of each language learning career . . . and the multitude of ways which can lead to success' (*ibid.*:70). In other words, each learner develops strategies and techniques which suit his or her individual needs and personality and implements these in different ways. Because of this, a definitive list of language learning strategies did not emerge, but the findings do allow certain generalisations, regardless of learner differences. Many of the characteristics and strategies identified overlapped and we have summarised them into the seven broad categories below. This categorisation was based on the conviction, supported by our own experience in the classroom, that it would make sense to the learners and therefore be appropriate as a basis for structuring a course of learner training.

As far as it is possible to generalise, good language learners are:

*self aware*
They are aware of and understand the reasons for their attitudes and feelings towards language learning and themselves as language learners. These attitudes are not necessarily positive, for example:

> 'I hate learning English grammar because I think it's illogical.'

> 'I don't enjoy speaking English because I'm afraid of making mistakes.'

*inquisitive and tolerant*
They are interested in finding out more about how the language works and how they can apply this knowledge to help them learn more effectively; for example:

> 'How is English grammar different from Italian grammar?'

> 'How many varieties of English are there and where are they spoken?'

They are also prepared to accept differences between their mother tongue and the target language and to tolerate ambiguity and uncertainty.

*self-critical*
They assess themselves and monitor their progress regularly.

*realistic*
They realise that it takes a lot of hard work and time to learn a foreign language and set themselves realistic, manageable short-term aims to make their learning easier to manage and to see their progress. This can also help them to remain motivated.

*willing to experiment*
They are willing to try out different learning strategies and practice activities and choose those that suit them best.

*actively involved*
They actively involve themselves in language learning and have sufficient

confidence not to mind experimenting with the language and taking risks.

*organised*
They organise their time and materials in ways which suit them personally and fully exploit the language learning resources available to them inside and outside the classroom.

Although this research has provided us with useful insights into what possibly makes for successful language learning, we believe there are dangers inherent in taking these findings too literally. If we are not careful, the resulting learner training course may become so prescriptive that it defeats its aim of encouraging learners to discover what works best for them as individuals. Furthermore, how should we define 'good' or 'successful'? One individual's interpretation may differ from that of another. In addition, learners presented with such a list could feel overwhelmed by what may seem to be an unattainable ideal; this could lead to anxiety and demotivation.

In our view, although the 'good language learner' research can provide a basis for devising a course of learner training, such a course needs to address the above-mentioned problems (see page 10).

## Learner training and materials

As already mentioned, another reason why learner training still remains a secondary concern in many language classrooms may be that there are relatively few learner training materials and guidelines for teachers on the market.

Dickinson and Carver (1980) identified three areas in which learners need preparation for learner autonomy, and which have also provided us with useful criteria for devising materials for learner training. These were:

*psychological preparation*, e.g. activities to build confidence for experimenting with language;

*methodological preparation*, e.g. activities to help learners understand and use metalanguage (language for describing language and language learning) and to become aware of the rationale behind classroom activities, such as pair work and drilling;

*practice in self-direction*, e.g. activities which provide learners with opportunities to make choices about their learning.

More recently it has been interesting to see how some aspects of learner training have begun to appear in published EFL and ESL materials

(Whitney 1983 and 1985, Prowse and McGrath 1984, McDowell and Hart 1987, among others).

## Learner training and the language learner

Learners bring into the classroom their own expectations about language learning, their teacher's role and their own roles. These expectations are often the result of past learning experiences and cultural background. Learner training can help learners of any age understand what is happening in the classroom and why. It may, however, be helpful to examine separately the problems of adults and younger learners.

### Adult learners

Many adults returning to the classroom to learn a foreign language have come from a past learning experience which concentrated on studying grammar and structures and provided few opportunities to use the language as a means of communication. Consequently, these learners may find it difficult to come to terms with more learner-centred and communicative approaches and teachers may hear such comments as 'I don't see the point of talking to other students in pairs.' or 'Why don't you correct all our mistakes?'

It may be that many adults have already made several attempts to learn a foreign language, but each time have given up – perhaps because of an apparent lack of progress, or dissatisfaction with the classes, materials or teacher. Although they have specific needs, they often set themselves unrealistic aims. This, combined with their false expectations about methodology and their own progress, can lead to frustration, demotivation and ineffective learning. Furthermore, adult learners, upon returning to the classroom, often revert to the 'traditional' role of pupil who expects to be told what to do as well as how and when to do it. They expect the teacher to control all aspects of learning and, in so doing, relinquish the autonomy they would normally exert in other spheres of their lives. Learner training aims to restore to learners the control they exercise outside the classroom so that they may be in a position to manage their learning according to their individual preferences and needs.

### Younger learners

Pupils starting to learn a foreign language are often highly motivated, but this initial interest tends to fade very quickly for a variety of reasons. Because of the constraints of many secondary school systems, such as a specific syllabus to cover, large classes, and limited time available for language learning, pupils are rarely given the opportunity to reflect on and make choices about their own learning. Furthermore, younger learners are sometimes self-conscious in class, have short concentration spans, are easily bored and rarely see the wider relevance of learning a foreign language. Learner training can be beneficial for the following reasons:

— it can help learners maintain their initial motivation by encouraging them to become more actively and personally involved in their own learning, and by helping them build up their confidence and to perceive progress;
— learners are in a position where they can transfer their knowledge about learning to other subjects across the curriculum;
— it can help to prevent the 'adult learner syndrome' described above.

## Learner training and language level

Although it may be dangerous to make assumptions about learners' levels of awareness about language learning, and diagnoses can sometimes be misleading, we have found that language learners who could be described as 'advanced', that is post Cambridge First Certificate level, are probably already aware of which learning strategies work well for them. In our experience, learner training is most effective at lower-intermediate level, as the learners are usually able to complete activities in the target language, which provides additional language work, and already have some language learning experience to reflect on. At the same time, they are at a relatively early stage in their learning of English, where they may benefit from knowledge about language learning and about themselves as language learners.

As discussion is widely accepted to be an important technique in learner training, it may be preferable for lower-level learners to complete some of the discussion-based activities in their mother tongue or another common language. Experience has shown that there is no loss of the learner training benefits if the target language is not used. Discussion can take place in any language (s) learners feel comfortable in, although obviously at some point the whole group needs to have the use of a common language.

The more advanced your learners are in terms of language level and learning awareness, the less learner training they are generally likely to need; in this case it is important to negotiate and be selective. At this level learner training is more likely to be targeted at specific, more sophisticated, language learning or practice tasks, such as writing an academic paper, business report or school essay.

## Learner training and the teacher's role

Many teachers have always been aware of the importance of helping learners 'learn how to learn' and have attempted to expand their roles to include not only language teaching but also aspects of learner training, as previously mentioned (see page 3). However, our investigations (Ellis and Sinclair, 1987) have shown that this is not always implemented in a principled and systematic way. In a systematic approach the teacher would play an instrumental role in learner training by:

— negotiating with learners about course content and methodology, if appropriate
— sharing with learners, in a way which is accessible to them, the kind of information about language and language learning that teachers have, but which is not always passed on to learners
— encouraging discussion in the classroom about language and language learning
— helping learners become aware of the wide range of alternative strategies available to them for language learning
— creating a learning environment where learners feel they can experiment with their language learning
— allowing learners to form their own conclusions about language learning and respecting individual points of view
— counselling and giving guidance to individual learners when possible.

The learner training in this book is partly teacher directed and partly learner directed. It is teacher directed in that the teacher provides much of the input about the language and about the learning process and presents alternative strategies — if the learners do not suggest these themselves — for experimentation and evaluation. The teacher is not intended to be prescriptive, however, and, in this respect, the *outcome* of the learner training is *learner directed*. It is the learner who decides which alternatives to adopt or reject.

The learner is regarded as an individual whose opinions and beliefs about learning are respected. He or she is encouraged to experiment and to choose and is provided with the necessary tools with which to do this. Learner and teacher are partners in learning; the teacher is the language learning 'expert' and the learner the 'expert' on him or herself.

Finally it is important to realise that no matter how principled and systematic the learner training may be, it is a gradual process and the teacher should not expect instant results. The main purpose of a learner training course is to *start* the learners on their own journeys towards self-knowledge and self-reliance.

# 2   Learning to Learn English

## The framework

| Stage 1  *Preparation for language learning* | |
| --- | --- |
| 1.1  What do you expect from your course? | |
| 1.2  What sort of language learner are you? | |
| 1.3  Why do you need or want to learn English? | |
| 1.4  How do you organise your learning? | |
| 1.5  How motivated are you? | |
| 1.6  What can you do in a self-access centre? | |

| Stage 2   *Skills training* | *How do you feel . . .?* | *What do you know . . .?* | *How well are you doing?* | *What do you need to do next?* | *How do you prefer to learn/practise . . .?* | *Do you need to build up your confidence?* | *How do you organise . . .?* |
| --- | --- | --- | --- | --- | --- | --- | --- |
| *Skills* | *Step 1* | *Step 2* | *Step 3* | *Step 4* | *Step 5* | *Step 6* | *Step 7* |
| 2.1  Extending vocabulary | | | | | | | |
| 2.2  Dealing with grammar | | | | | | | |
| 2.3  Listening | | | | | | | |
| 2.4  Speaking | | | | | | | |
| 2.5  Reading | | | | | | | |
| 2.6  Writing | | | | | | | |

*Learning to Learn English* provides a framework for a course of learner training. It consists of two stages which together form a syllabus as follows:

*Stage 1    Preparation for language learning*
*Stage 2    Skills training*

The two stages provide a carefully sequenced progression of activities (see the diagram on page 11).

Stage 1 and part of Stage 2 contain activities which develop what O'Malley et al. (1985a:24) describe as metacognitive strategies, that is, they involve the learners in *reflecting on the learning process*, planning for learning, self-assessment and monitoring. Metacognitive strategies may, in fact, be applied to all types of learning.

Stage 2 contains a mixture of metacognitive strategies and what O'Malley et al. (*ibid.*) call cognitive strategies, that is, those more directly related to specific learning tasks, which involve the learners in *doing things with the language and their learning materials* (rather than just thinking). These differ according to the subject to be learnt and the nature of the learning task. For example, although metacognitive strategies for learning a language are the same as for learning tap dancing, the cognitive strategies are very different.

Experiments we have carried out (Ellis and Sinclair 1986b) have demonstrated that courses which focussed on both metacognitive and cognitive strategy development tended to produce more positive feedback from the learners than courses which focussed on only one of these aspects. In addition, it has been suggested that the combination of metacognitive with cognitive strategy development makes it easier for learners to transfer strategy training to other learning tasks. As O'Malley et al. state (*op.cit.*:24), 'Students without metacognitive approaches are essentially learners without direction and ability to review their progress, accomplishments and future learning directions'.

On the other hand, training learners in metacognitive strategies only is denying them the opportunity for active experimentation with their learning.

As far as possible, the activities in Stage 2 incorporate reflection and experimentation in the following sequence:

reflection   →   experimentation   →   reflection

O'Malley et al.(*ibid.*) also refer to a third type of learning strategy, which they call 'social-mediating' or 'socioaffective', which involves learners in co-operating together in language learning activities. We have chosen not to include in this book activities which focus solely on developing collaborative learning strategies; we have found it more economical, natural and effective to integrate this aspect of learning into the types of activities already described, where appropriate. The activities which do this are indicated by the following symbols in the Learner's Book:

Throughout the book learners from around the world give their points of view about language learning and learning strategies. This is intended to emphasise the fact that each language learner is an individual and that there are many different learning strategies which can lead to success. For these reasons, we believe that all points of view should be regarded as valid and presenting them contributes to a non-prescriptive approach to learner training.

### Reading lists

At the end of this Introduction, some of the sections in Stage 1 and each skill in Stage 2 you will find a reading list containing references to books or articles that we have found helpful. It is broken down into two sections:

*Further reading*: contains references which you may like to follow up in order to obtain more detailed information about some of the issues raised. They consist mainly of teachers' handbooks and articles.

*Recommended for learners*: contains references to materials that could be used with your learners in class or that they could use for self-study.

Full publication details are contained in the bibliography at the end of the book.

### Stage 1  Preparation for language learning

This stage contains six sections and aims to prepare learners for their language course and learner training by giving them opportunities to consider a variety of factors which may affect their language learning. At the same time, it provides learners and teachers with the necessary information for negotiating and planning suitable routes through Stage 2.

*1.1    What do you expect from your course?*
This section aims to help learners begin to clarify their expectations and feelings about their course and to discuss its aims and methodology with their teacher.

*1.2    What sort of language learner are you?*
Here learners begin the process of reflection on their own learning styles.

*1.3    Why do you need or want to learn English?*
This section aims to help learners analyse and prioritise their language needs and consider their long-term language learning aims.

*1.4   How do you organise your learning?*
This section encourages learners to find out about language learning resources available to them, to organise their materials in ways which suit them personally, to assess realistically the time available to them for language learning and to use this time efficiently by planning regular review sessions.

*1.5   How motivated are you?*
Here learners are encouraged to keep records of their motivation levels and to consider the factors that affect these. Strong motivation, personal determination and a willingness to persist are considered to be crucial factors in language learning, as reflected by the following comment from a young learner, '*Écouter les conseils qu'on vous donne, travailler et ne pas se désespérer quand ça ne va pas!*' (Cédric, aged 12). ('Listen to the advice you are given, work and don't get discouraged when things don't go well!')

*1.6   What can you do in a self-access centre?*
This is an optional section, depending on the facilities available in the learners' institution. It aims to help them become familiar with the self-access centre and aware of its potential as a resource for learning.

### Stage 2   Skills training

This stage of the framework is based on a series of seven *Steps* running horizontally and a series of six *skills* running vertically to form a grid. This structure allows each Step to be applied to each skill and produces 42 learner training components, as represented by the boxes in the grid. Each of these boxes contains a suggested checklist of items to cover (see pages 30–3).
   The skills contained in Stage 2 of the framework are:
     *Extending vocabulary*
     *Dealing with grammar*
     *Listening*
     *Speaking*
     *Reading*
     *Writing.*
*Extending vocabulary* and *Dealing with grammar* have been included as separate skills in order to reflect their importance and the preoccupation of many learners with these areas.
   The Steps are based on the seven categories (see pages 6–7) which we found provided a useful starting point for structuring Stage 2 of the framework. In order to avoid being prescriptive, we have transformed the seven categories into questions which form the basis for the learner training activities in this stage. In this way, the learners are given the opportunity to use a questioning approach and become more involved,

so that they are in a position to take on greater responsibility for managing their own learning.

The Steps are sequenced so that the learners begin by reflecting on themselves as language learners and on the language itself and, later on, experiment with a variety of learning strategies. In this way, they are involved in activities which increasingly require them to take on more responsibility for their own learning.

## Step 1   How do you feel . . . ?

Learners often have very definite opinions about what is right or wrong in language learning without understanding the reasons for these. The aim of Step 1 is to give them the opportunity to:
— examine a variety of different attitudes to language learning and teaching, including their own
— consider the implications of these attitudes for their own learning.
Your role is to encourage discussion and examination of learners' attitudes.

## Step 2   What do you know . . . ?

This Step aims to give learners basic knowledge that they can apply to their own language learning by providing specific language awareness information for each skill. Much of this information is of the type included in teacher training programmes, but is not often passed on to the learners in an accessible way. We believe that learners can benefit from being informed, as they may thus gain greater insight into the possible reasons for language learning problems.

The activities in this Step are generally more teacher-centred than those in the rest of the book and your main role at this point is that of informant.

## Step 3   How well are you doing?

This Step aims to train learners to assess their own linguistic performance and so be in a position to take on responsibility for monitoring their progress.

Your role is to provide learners with clear guidance in establishing criteria for self-assessment and regular opportunities for discussing self-assessment.

## Step 4   What do you need to do next?

This Step encourages learners to set themselves short-term aims as markers of progress.

Learners are often very unrealistic about how much they can learn in the time available. For those with a limited amount of time, learning to set realistic short-term aims is very important.

Your role is to encourage learners to discuss and establish their own learning priorities and to be prepared to re-negotiate course content, if appropriate.

### Step 5    How do you prefer to learn/practise . . . ?

The aim of this Step is to encourage learners to consider the potential of a variety of learning strategies and identify those which suit them best.

Learners are often not aware of the wide range of strategies at their disposal and may be making use of only a very limited number; these may not be the ones most suited to them or their learning styles.

Your role is to encourage learners to experiment with and reflect on different learning strategies.

### Step 6    Do you need to build up your confidence?

This Step aims to:
— increase learners' confidence so that they are better equipped to cope with situations that require experimentation
— encourage learners to use an active approach to language learning and to become less afraid of making mistakes.

Some learners are reluctant to experiment in any way. This may be due, for example, to personality, cultural background, or past learning experiences. There is also evidence to suggest that some effective language learners prefer to listen quietly for a time while others are talking. While it is not the intention of this Step to force learners into a situation where they may feel uncomfortable, we have found that if the teacher can create a stress-free language learning environment, learners generally feel less anxious about experimenting. For these learners, we suggest that the first Step 6 you cover is in the skill of listening or reading.

Some learners may already be confident language users. It is important not to let them intimidate other members of the class. If necessary, speak to these learners in private and impress upon them that all class members should have equal opportunities to practise (Bruce and Ellis 1987).

### Step 7    How do you organise . . . ?

The aim of this Step is to help learners become aware of a variety of ways of organising their work and select those they prefer.

Your role is to encourage an exchange of ideas and to advise and inform where necessary, without being prescriptive.

The framework for Stage 2 is flexible in that it may be worked through horizontally, Step by Step, for one skill at a time, or vertically, focussing on one Step at a time for several skills.

**Selecting skills**

In 1.3 learners prioritise the skills they need or want to improve and this provides the basis for selecting the skills to cover in Stage 2.

**Selecting steps**

If this is the first time your learners are doing learner training, we recommend that they should cover each of the seven Steps at least once in the sequence we have suggested. If they are familiar with learner training they may not need to cover every Step for each skill. The strategies and techniques they have developed, or are developing, should be referred to and adapted in an on-going process throughout their learning career. The components to be selected from Stage 2 of the learner training programme can, of course, be negotiated and agreed with your learners.

The diagram on page 11 can be used for recording the components you are going to cover during the learner training course.

## The learner training activities

How is a learner training activity different from a language learning activity? The learner training activities in this book have three features which distinguish them from language learning activities:

1. They focus on the learning *process* rather than on what is learnt.
2. They are 'informed' rather than 'blind' (Wenden 1986b:316). An 'informed' activity is one where the learners are aware of its aims so that they realise why a particular strategy can be helpful. If the activity leaves the learners in the dark about its importance or relevance then it is 'blind'. For example, a teacher who was training her class in strategies for guessing unknown words by inserting some made-up words in a text, received the following comment from a learner: 'What is the point of learning imaginary words when there are so many real words we don't know in English?' This is a typical example of a learner misunderstanding the aims of an activity. The comment could have been pre-empted had the learner been properly informed of the rationale behind the learner training activity (see *2.5 Reading* Step 6 (2)).
3. They have an *outcome*. If an activity is 'informed', it follows that there must be a useful outcome and that the learner is not left thinking, 'What was all that about, then?'

Learner training activities can have two types of outcome:

i) *reflection*
ii) *reflection and experimentation*

On this basis, we can divide the learner training activities in the Learner's Book into two categories:

| *Type* (i) | *Type* (ii) |
|---|---|
| Learner training activities providing opportunities for *reflection* e.g. *1.1 What do you expect from your course?* (page 38) | Learner training activities providing opportunities for *reflection and experimentation* e.g. *2.1 Extending vocabulary* (page 62) |
| *Focus* | |
| relate to language learning or skills areas in *general*, e.g. thinking about past learning experiences, attitudes towards speaking | relate to specific activities or strategies in specific skills areas, e.g. reading for gist, improving fluency |
| *Implementation* | |
| lend themselves to being introduced as:<br>– induction sessions at the start of a new course<br>– separate learner training sessions | lend themselves to being integrated systematically into the language learning syllabus, i.e. they can either lead into or follow on from language learning activities in the classroom |
| *Language used* | |
| can be carried out in the learners' mother tongue without any loss of the learner training benefits | are usually carried out in the target language and so provide extra language input and fluency practice |
| *Activity type* | |
| usually take the form of:<br>– discussion activities<br>– questionnaires<br>– quizzes | provide a wide variety of activity types, e.g. problem-solving, guessing, comparing, role play |
| *Strategy type* | |
| encourage development of metacognitive learning strategies | encourage development of metacognitive and cognitive learning strategies |

## How to plan a timetable

The amount of learner training to be included in a course will depend not only on the aims of the learners and their language level (see page 9) but also on the length and type of the course.

### Intensive courses

We have found that on intensive courses it is generally appropriate to include a greater proportion of learner training activities than on extensive courses. This is because maximum use needs to be made of the course time available so that the learners are in a position to carry on learning after the course has finished.

On page 21 you will find an example of a timetable devised for a 30 hour, one-week intensive course for German adult learners at lower-intermediate level, whose aims were to improve their speaking and listening skills. A communicative approach was used and materials specially produced for the language learning activities. Each learner was counselled before the course and told that part of it would be concerned with learning how to learn. As can be seen from the timetable, learner training constituted approximately 30% of the course content (i.e. about nine hours). This proportion was found to be the most effective after three years of experimentation and monitoring of learner feedback on such courses.

### Extensive courses

In comparison, we found that for an extensive course of the same number of hours (three hours per week for ten weeks), the appropriate proportion of learner training was approximately 10–15% of the course content (see Fig. 2). This is because, generally speaking, learners on extensive courses tended to have course books which they could use out of class as a dependable source of input and which they wanted to complete. They also felt less need to be independent. On such courses, after the induction phase, learner training activities may need to be integrated into the language classes in a more gradual manner as the learners are less likely to perceive themselves as needing such training so urgently.

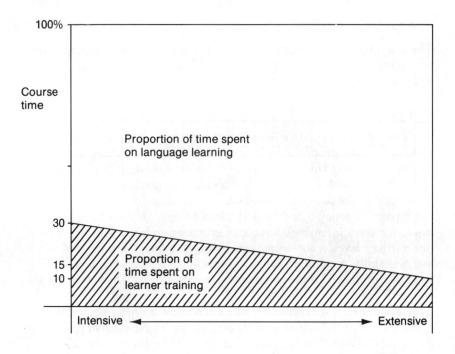

*Figure 2*

For extensive courses, we would suggest integrating learner training into the language learning activities as far as possible. For example, for multilingual classes of young adult European learners, on an 80 hour course over four weeks (five hours a day for four days a week) in Britain, we found a total of approximately one hour a day integrated into language work effective in helping them discover strategies for continuing to learn independently when back in their own countries. For French secondary school pupils aged 11–14 who were having three hours of English a week, we found about ten minutes of learner training integrated into a lesson was appropriate.

**One week intensive English language course** (30 hours)   Level: lower-intermediate

| Time | Monday | Tuesday | Wednesday | Thursday | Friday |
|---|---|---|---|---|---|
| 8.30 – 10.00 | 'Breaking the ice!' (Getting to know each other) | * How to improve your discussion techniques<br><br>*Stage 2: 2.4 Speaking Step 2* | * How to talk about the past:<br><br>*Stage 2: 2.2 Grammar Steps 3, 4* | * How to improve your social skills | Language recycling (Video) |
| 10.15 – 11.30 | † Preparation for language learning<br><br>*Stage 1: 1.1, 1.2, 1.5* | Practising your discussion techniques: role play | Role play and feedback | * Role plays and feedback | * It's your choice (Self-access revision)<br><br>*Stage 2: 2.2 Grammar Step 4*<br>*2.3 Listening Step 4*<br>*2.4 Speaking Step 4* |
| 11.45 – 12.30 | † Grammar: Typical mistakes of German speakers<br><br>*Stage 2: 2.2 Grammar Steps 1, 2, 3, 4* | * Assessment and feedback<br><br>*Stage 2: 2.4 Speaking Steps 3, 4* | Grammar clinic | Grammar clinic | Feedback and 'round-up' |
| 14.00 – 15.15 | How to talk about the future: plans, intentions, business appointments | † How to improve your listening techniques<br><br>*Stage 2: 2.3 Listening Steps 1, 2, 6* | * How to be more fluent<br><br>*Stage 2: 2.4 Speaking Step 6* | * Be creative in English! (Radio or TV programme) | |
| 15.30 – 16.30 | * How to improve your telephoning techniques<br><br>*Stage 2: 2.4 Speaking Steps 1, 2, 3, 5* | † How to extend your vocabulary<br><br>*Stage 2: 2.1 Vocabulary Steps 1, 2, 5, 6* | † Let's debate! | * Feedback and assessment | |

Learner training = approximately 9 hours (30%)

* = Learner training integrated into classwork
† = Learner training in separate sessions

21

## How to plan a learner training lesson

*The checklists*

At the beginning of each section in Stage 1 and each Step in Stage 2 you will find a checklist which provides the following information to facilitate your preparation:

*Materials*
The relevant pages in the Learner's Book are indicated. You are also told if you need to use the cassette or any other materials or aids, such as topic cards, newspapers, dictionaries.

*Items to cover*
This provides a summary of the contents of the section or Step. In addition, pages 29–33 provide an overview of the contents of Stages 1 and 2.

*Time*
Suggested timings have been provided for each section or Step. However, these timings are only approximate, as they will depend on a number of factors, such as the language level of your learners, their level of awareness about language learning, their needs and interests, the time you have available for language learning and your syllabus, and the order in which you cover the skills. You may also decide you do not need to cover all of the activities in each section or Step.

*Lesson planning*

We suggest the following procedure for planning your lessons:

1. Start from your language learning materials, that is the language learning aims of your lesson (perhaps the aims for a particular unit of the course book you are using).
2. Bearing in mind, as far as possible, the sequencing of the Steps, assess your teaching materials for their learner training potential. In other words, which items from the checklist of a particular learner training component could you most usefully integrate?
3. Read the notes in the Teacher's Book relating to items you want to cover and decide where in your lesson the learner training could best be introduced and how much time you estimate you will need for it.

We have found it helpful to use a lesson planning sheet like the one on page 23. Notice that the objectives are ordered so that learner training is the last item to be considered. We have found that this prevents the learner training in Stage 2 from overriding the language learning aims of a lesson, and allows it to be derived naturally from and incorporated into language work. The ordering of the other objectives may vary according

LESSON PLANNING SHEET

Date: 17. 3. 86

Class: 4ème (age 13-14 yrs - 3rd year of English)

Length of lesson: 50 mins.

Materials: ~~Imagine You're English 4~~, Chapter 8, page 44, Belin, 1974. ~~Learning to Learn English~~, Stage 2.3, Step 2.

Objectives

| | |
|---|---|
| Structural | 'Can' used for ability, possibility and permission. Imperative: turn left, go straight on, etc. Future 'will': you'll find, you'll see, etc. |
| Functional | Understanding directions. Attracting attention. Asking for and giving directions. |
| Skills | Listening to native speakers of English. Speaking. |
| Phonological | Understanding the pronunciation of stressed and weak forms in spoken English. |
| Lexical | Place names in London. Lexis for directions. |
| Learner training | Information about listening to English. English is a stress-timed language. 100% comprehension is not necessary. |
| Anticipated difficulties | Information about listening to English – probably on overload of English, so will use the class's mother tongue (French). Tight on time! |

Evaluation: Pupils appreciated Stage 3 (glad I did it in French). They especially liked the rhythms we built up!

PROCEDURES

| Time | | Activity | Aids |
|---|---|---|---|
| of lesson | of each stage | | |
| 9.00<br><br><br><br><br><br><br>9.05 | <br><br><br><br><br><br><br>5 | 1. <u>Introduction/Motivation</u><br>T shows pupils a picture of a tourist and a police officer in London and elicits possible topics of conversation to set scene.<br>T states aims of lesson:<br>Understanding directions.<br>Asking for and giving directions. | Picture |
| 9.10 | 5 | 2. <u>Marie-Claude's problems</u><br>T plays cassette of Marie-Claude from LLE and elicits possible problems.<br>T asks pupils to consider their own problems when listening to English. | Cassette |
| 9.25 | 15 | 3. <u>Information about listening</u><br>T explains that English is stress-timed following instructions on page 95 of Teacher's Book of LLE. | Cassette BB |
| 9.30<br><br><br><br><br>9.40<br><br><br><br><br><br><br>9.50 | 5<br><br><br><br><br>10<br><br><br><br><br><br><br>10 | 4. <u>Focus on language</u>: Asking for & giving directions.<br><u>Presentation</u>: Pupils listen to cassette of native speaker giving directions & they follow on map.<br><u>Controlled Practice</u>: T-class practise asking for directions using page 44 of "Imagine You're English 4".<br><u>Production</u>: Role play. T distributes cue cards with a given destination, e.g. The National Gallery. Pupil A asks directions and Pupil B gives directions - using street map. Pairs change over, and then pupil A moves on to form a new pair with another pupil. | Cassette |

to the focus of your language materials, for example depending on whether they are structurally-based or functionally-based. The lesson plan on pages 23–4 is for a class of French secondary school pupils, aged 13–14, using a structurally-based course book and incorporating learner training components for listening. (You will find a blank lesson planning sheet which you can copy for your own use on page 145 of this book.)

## How to prepare your learners

However learner training is implemented, it is essential that the learners are fully informed about the intention to include learner training in their course, so that they do not perceive time spent on it as time lost for language learning. This can be done by providing information about learner training in course descriptions or brochures (see page 26) or by discussing it with prospective students during pre-course counselling or placement procedures. In a French secondary school, learner training took the form of a project entitled 'Learning to learn English'. The pupils were each given a project folder which stated the aims of the project (see page 27) and in which they were able to organise their work related to learner training. This made the learner training more explicit and helped the pupils see it as an ongoing process.

Preparation of this kind can help to prevent any mismatch of expectations and resistance to learner training.

## What do learners think about learner training?

Due to the constraints of most teaching situations, it can be difficult to evaluate empirically the effects of a learner training course in terms of learning strategies. However, as teachers, we have observed changes in learners' attitudes towards language learning, as well as the development of a more active and personal involvement in their own learning during their courses. Feedback collected at the end of courses over a period of three years has confirmed an overall positive response. Here are some learners' comments:

1. 'I'm really enjoying this course. I'm discovering and learning how I can improve my English communication. [ . . . ] the most important thing is that I have to try to expressing myself, in the best way but I should be calm. I should forget I get nervous when I speak in English. This course helps us to recognize our problems, and to get a solution to success them.' *Cecilia*

2. 'I've been taking this course for about five or six Saturdays and I'm really happy to be taken it. The course is very interesting and it has helped me to find out how to improve my English. It gave me the opportunitie to evaluate my English knowledge, to recognize my

⋙→ *p.28*

# 1 WEEK
# INTENSIVE COURSE

**Level:** Lower-intermediate
**Hours:** 30

**Aim:** This course aims to help you develop your knowledge of the English language in general, to improve your understanding of natural spoken English and to increase your confidence and fluency in speaking the language. The course will introduce you to a variety of ways of learning and practising English and help you to develop your own strategies for continuing to learn after the course.

**Content:** As well as activities which are designed to improve your understanding of spoken English and your fluency, your grammatical problems will be diagnosed and covered in special sessions. There will also be special sessions of 'learner training', which aim to help you discover ways of learning English which are best for you. For example, you will have a look at how to increase your vocabulary.

**Activities:** The course will include activities where you work in pairs or groups with other students, listening to cassettes, watching videos, using the computers, role play, games and making a video film, etc. A qualified and experienced teacher whose mother tongue is English will be with you at all times to help, advise and teach you.

PROJECT 1987

## LEARNING TO LEARN ENGLISH

A chacun sa façon d'apprendre. Notre objectif
est de vous aider à découvrir personnellement
le meilleur moyen d'apprendre l'anglais.
Apprendre à apprendre c'est ce que nous
appelons le 'learner training'.

Vous utiliserez ce dossier avec votre manuel
d'anglais. En classe vous échangerez avec vos
camarades vos idées sur l'apprentissage des
langues étrangères afin de partager vos
différentes expériences.

(Everybody learns in a different way. Our aim is to
help you discover the best way for you to learn
English. Learning how to learn is called 'learner
training'.
  You will use this project with your English
coursebook. In class you will discuss your ideas
about learning foreign languages with the other
pupils so that you may learn from each other.)

priorities and mistakes, and when I heard about the problems of the other students I learned new things.'   *Alicia*

Lower-intermediate learners in Lima, Peru. Average age of the class: 22.

3.  'I think this course gave me an idea to learn better.'   *Sabine*

4.  'I got new techniques for a more effective learning and useful hints to correct myself.'   *Günter*

Lower-intermediate adult learners after a one-week intensive course in Munich, Germany.

5.  'Les leçons sont très intéressantes et elles m'ont appris des choses que je ne savais pas sur moi et sur l'anglais.'
    (The lessons are very interesting and they have taught me a lot of things that I didn't know about myself and English.)   *Wilfried*

6.  'On peut parler en anglais, on est plus libre et on fait des progrès mutuellement en essayant de se comprendre.'
    (We can speak in English, we are freer and we make progress together, trying to understand each other.)   *Aurélie*

Pupils in their first year of English at secondary school in Paris, France.

STAGE 1

---

**1.1  What do you expect from your course?**
Language learning, accuracy and fluency, course aims and methodology, role of the teacher, introduction to learner training.

---

**1.2  What sort of language learner are you?**
Quiz: learning styles, suggestions for becoming a more effective learner.

---

**1.3  Why do you need or want to learn English?**
1. *Analysing your needs*
2. *Prioritising your needs*

---

**1.4  How do you organise your learning?**
1. *Have you got a dictionary?*
2. *Have you got a grammar book?*
3. *What other resources have you got?*
4. *How do you organise your materials?*
5. *How much time have you got to learn English?*
6. *How do you organise your time?*

---

**1.5  How motivated are you?**
How motivation can affect learning.
How to keep a motivation graph.

---

**1.6  What can you do in a self-access centre?**
1. *In class:* discussion
2. *In the self-access centre:* research
3. *Time to experiment*
4. *One learner's experience*
5. *Keeping records*

---

| | Step 1 | Step 2 | Step 3 | Step 4 | Step 5 | Step 6 | Step 7 |
|---|---|---|---|---|---|---|---|
| **2.1 Extending vocabulary** | Learners' attitudes towards vocabulary | *Active and passive vocabulary*<br>2. *Knowing a word* | *Introduction*<br>1. *Points to assess*<br>2. *Test yourself in a practice activity*<br>3. *Assess your performance in a real-life situation*<br>4. *Examples* | *Introduction* Setting short-term aims | *Personal strategies* Learning new words<br>2. *Time to experiment –* Grouping words Common features Word network<br>3. *Time to experiment –* Making associations Word bag Word tour Word clip<br>4. *Choose a new strategy* | *What can you do when you don't know a word?* Shopping | |

**EXAMPLES** (between Step 3 and Step 4 region)

**EXAMPLES** (Step 7 region)

| | | Points to assess | EXAMPLES | |
|---|---|---|---|---|
| **2.2 Dealing with grammar** | Learners' attitudes towards grammar | 1. *Languages are different* 2. *What is grammar?* Facts, patterns and choices Using a pattern | 1. *Points to assess* 2. *Test yourself in a practice activity* 3. *Assess your performance in a real-life situation* 4. *Examples* | 1. *Personal strategies* 2. *Suggestions* Pattern Banks Discuss grammar 3. *Choose a new strategy* | *Discovering the pattern or rule* Some and any The human computer |

| | | Points to assess | EXAMPLES | |
|---|---|---|---|---|
| **2.3 Listening** | Learners' attitudes towards listening | 1. *Listening to native-speakers of English* Stress-timed language Guessing what a conversation is about 2. *Listening strategies* Listening for gist, selecting and rejecting Reasons for listening | 1. *Points to assess* 2. *Test yourself in a practice activity* 3. *Assess your performance in a real-life situation* 4. *Examples* | 1. *Personal strategies* 2. *Time to experiment* How to take control 3. *Choose a new strategy* | 1. *Preparing and predicting* Listening to the news 2. *How we predict* Can you predict in English? |

31

| | Step 1 | Step 2 | Step 3 | Step 4 | Step 5 | Step 6 | Step 7 |
|---|---|---|---|---|---|---|---|
| | | | | EXAMPLES | | | EXAMPLES |
| **2.4 Speaking** | Learners' attitudes towards speaking | 1. English as a world language 2. Pronunciation 3. Stress Syllables Words in sentences 4. Intonation 5. Features of spoken English | 1. Points to assess Focus on accuracy Focus on fluency Describing a photograph Recording yourself 2. Test yourself in a practice activity 3. Assess your performance in a real-life situation 4. Examples | | 1. Personal strategies 2. Time to experiment Problem solving 3. Choose a new strategy | 1. Thinking-time techniques Just a Minute! 2. Suggestions | |
| **2.5 Reading** | Learners' attitudes towards reading | 1. Reading speed 2. Reading strategies Skimming, scanning and reading for detail Reading a menu | 1. Points to assess 2. Test yourself in a practice activity 3. Assess your performance in a real-life situation 4. Examples | | 1. Personal strategies 2. Suggestions 3. Choose a new strategy | 1. Predicting Completing sentences 2. Guessing unknown words Guessing out of context Guessing in context | |

## 2.6 Writing

Learners' attitudes towards writing

Discover the useful tip

EXAMPLES

| EXAMPLES | EXAMPLES |
|---|---|
| 1. What do people write? Writing for communication and personal writing | 1. Points to assess Invent your own marking scheme Marking an essay |
| 2. Characteristics of written texts Comparing written texts | 2. Test yourself in a practice activity |
| 3. What are the features of a well-written text? Detective work | 3. Assess your performance in a real-life situation |
|  | 4. Examples |

| EXAMPLES |
|---|
| Writing spontaneously Dictation Timed writing |
| 1. Personal strategies |
| 2. Time to experiment Writing drafts Class guide Create a magazine |
| 3. Suggestions Model Banks Memorise |
| 4. Choose a new strategy |

33

## Further reading

Aitchison, J. 1983. An introduction to psycholinguistics.

Altman, H.B. and James, C.V. (eds.) 1980. A collection of studies from different countries which aim to adapt language courses to the needs of individual learners.

Bialystok, E. 1985. This article discusses the relationship between L2 teaching and learning strategies, excluding those involved in communication, discourse, language perception and language production.

British Council 1978. A collection of papers which illustrate different opinions and approaches to individualisation in language learning.

Bruce, K. and Ellis, G. 1987. This article examines the extent to which sex differences in communicative competence are transferred to the mixed-sex foreign language classroom where a communicative approach is used, and concludes with a list of suggestions to enable the teacher to help promote equal opportunities for all students to practise.

Carroll, J.B. 1967. This essay lays out research problems about young children's second language learning from the standpoint of the world scene, with recognition of the many different linguistic situations that present themselves from one country or region to another.

Crookall, D. 1983. These articles argue that learner training is a neglected yet worthwhile teaching strategy and describes a game as a way of providing students with an initiation to EFL methodology.

Dickinson, L. and Carver, D. 1980. This article examines why learners find it difficult to become autonomous in language learning. It suggests three aspects of preparation that learners need in order to come to terms with the complexity of language learning and shows how familiar language teaching and learning techniques can be used to give this preparation.

Dickinson, L. 1987. This book explores the many ways in which teachers can help their students become more independent in their language learning.

Ellis, G. and Sinclair, B. 1986a. This paper argues that for learner training to be successful it needs to be carried out systematically, and presents a model of learner training for teachers who wish to include this in their teaching.

Ellis, G. and Sinclair, B. 1986b. This is an account of a presentation given at the 1986 IATEFL Brighton conference which described the application of a model for a systematic programme of learner training in two settings: a secondary school in Paris and the British Council in Munich with adult learners.

Ellis, G. and Sinclair, B. 1987. An account of a presentation given at the 1987 IATEFL Westende conference. It investigated some of the problems that confront teachers who wish to implement learner training, and then hypothesised that if they experienced learner training as part of a teacher training course, they might become more confident and successful learner trainers.

Freire, P. 1972. This book argues that education can only be liberating if it avoids authoritarian teacher-pupil models and is based on the actual experiences of students and on continual shared investigation.

Fröhlich, M. and Paribakht, T. 1984. A review of three studies carried out in the Modern Language Centre of the Ontario Institute for Studies in Education between 1975 and 1982 to examine how good learners succeed in learning one or more languages.

Geddes, M. and Sturtridge, G. (eds.) 1982. A special issue of *Modern English Teacher* magazine containing thirteen articles on different aspects and applications of individualised learning.

Gomes de Matos, F. 1986. This article argues that despite progress achieved in education, a gap still exists in descriptive-explanatory frameworks for second language learning and teaching: that of language learners' rights.

Grandcolas, B. 1986. This article describes an experiment carried out with trainee teachers of French as a foreign language at the Université de Paris VIII. As part of their course, they learnt a new foreign language and kept a learning diary in order to sensitise them to factors affecting their learning, methodology, use of the mother tongue, learning strategies, etc.

Grandcolas, B. and Soulé-Susbielles, N. 1986. This article argues that the foreign language classroom is an important arena for educational and linguistic research. It surveys research that has been conducted in France on the analysis of the foreign language classroom, and then discusses two research projects, one a diary study at the Université de Paris VIII and the other on classroom analysis by teachers and pupils.

Hallgarten, K. and Rostworowska, B. 1985. Learner training materials produced on the ALBSU Independent Learning project for ESL and literacy groups in adult education.

Harding-Esch, E. (ed.) 1976. A collection of eight papers representing a wide variety of continuing experimental work on autonomy and self-direction in second language learning.

Hassall, S. 1983. This paper describes a study carried out in Bahrain in 1982 which aimed to discover whether the conscious application by the student of the techniques and strategies used by 'good language learners' and made explicit by the teacher, would make any appreciable difference in achievement.

Higgs, D. 1985. This is the training manual focussing on learners which accompanies the British Council's *Teacher and Learning in Focus* series.

Holec, H. 1981. A theoretical and practical description of the application of the concept of autonomy in language learning.

Holec, H. 1988. A collection of papers which describe the methods and procedures that have been used in several European countries and in different educational sectors to develop the autonomy of students as language users and as language learners.

Illich, I. 1973. A collection of essays which discuss issues raised once the hypothesis that society can be deschooled is embraced.

Krashen, S. 1981. Krashen's 'Monitor Theory' of adult second language acquisition which hypothesises that adults have two independent systems for developing ability in second languages, subconscious language acquisition and conscious learning.

Littlejohn, A. 1985. An article which argues that a truly learner-centred approach to language education must provide opportunities for learner choice in the method and scope of study.

Littlewood, W. 1984. A survey of work done in the field of foreign and second language learning and its relevance for language teaching.

Marshall, L.A. and Rowland, F. 1983. This book is designed to help a wide range of students, including those beginning 6th form or college, those returning to study, and those starting full-time or part-time courses in adult education, to discover their own learning purposes and style by offering a range of ideas and techniques from which to choose.

McDowell, J. and Hart, C. 1987. Authentic recordings with tasks to develop listening skills and learner training.

Naiman, N. et al. 1978. A report on a two-year project which investigated the kinds of strategies and techniques successful adult learners employed, as well as the general learning conditions under which they acquired the new language and other factors contributing to their success.

Nisbet, J. and Shucksmith, J. 1986. A review and analysis of learning strategies of pupils in the Grampian Region, Scotland. The book aims to encourage teachers to start thinking about different approaches to harnessing the potential of young learners. It concludes by reviewing the place of learning strategies in the curriculum.

O'Malley, J.M. et al. 1985a. This article reports on a study designed to identify strategies that students can use to improve second language learning and retention.

O'Malley, J.M. et al. 1985b. This article reports on a study which was conducted with high school ESL students to identify the range and frequency of learning strategy uses and the effects of training in learning strategies on English language skills. The results are discussed in terms of implications for teaching and future research.

Oxford-Carpenter, R. 1985. A review of recent research findings on second language learning strategies.

Porter Ladousse, G. 1982. This article considers the limitations of some of the current theories of motivation in foreign language learning and then discusses Nuttin's dynamic interactional theory of motivation. The relevance of this theory to language learning and some of the pedagogical factors implied by it are discussed.

Prowse, P. and McGrath, I. 1984. A set of communicative course materials for post-intermediate learners of English containing sections on 'Skills for Studying English'.

Rivers, W.M. 1983. A collection of papers dealing with language learning theory, bilingualism and second language acquisition.

Rogers, C. 1969. This book discusses the development of a personal philosophy which sees the teacher as a facilitator in the learning process.

Rubin, J. 1975. This paper indicates what strategies successful language learners might use and it is suggested that teachers can begin to help their less successful students improve their performance by paying more attention to learning strategies already seen as productive.

Rubin, J. and Thompson, I. 1982. A guide for language learners based on recent research findings on learning strategies and good language learners.

Sinclair, B. and Ellis, G. 1984. This article describes a systematic approach towards promoting learner autonomy on a four-week intensive course for the European Youth Centre of the Council of Europe.

Skehan, P. forthcoming. This book surveys research on individual differences in second language learning. It covers language aptitude, motivation, learner strategies, personality variables, as well as interaction between learner type and methodology.

Stern, H.H. 1975. This paper discusses what it means to know and learn a language and draws up an inventory of features that mark out good language learning.

Stern, H.H. 1983. This work puts the various aspects of applied linguistic research into historical and inter-disciplinary perspective.

Stevick, E.W. 1982. An account of how teacher and students interact, how the mind deals with foreign language data, a description of techniques, and information about phonology and grammar.

Toney, T. 1983. A survey review of six guides for language learners published between 1965 and 1982.

Underhill, N. 1981. This paper considers how English as an International Language sees English mainly as a means of communication between non-native speakers and the implications of this for teaching methods and materials.

Wallace, M.J. 1980. A course in study skills for students in further and higher education institutions.

Wenden, A.L. 1985a. An article based on excerpts from an interview with a second language learner. Some of the findings are analysed to answer the questions, 'What prompts second language learners to use strategies?' and 'What is the significance of learner strategies?'

Wenden, A.L. 1985b. This paper considers the implications of research on learner strategies for the role of the second language teacher.

Wenden, A.L. 1986a. An analysis of semi-structured interviews of 34 adult language learners of ESL which revealed that they had explicit beliefs about how to learn a second language. A set of modules is described which was designed to help students 'think about learning' in order to discover their own beliefs and consider alternative views, and the educational value of such activities is discussed.

Wenden, A.L. 1986b. This paper suggests that learner training remains a secondary concern in many second language classrooms because of a lack of guidelines to direct a systematic approach in devising materials and activities for its implementation. It outlines a set of criteria that can be used to guide such attempts and illustrates their application in five ESL settings.

Wenden, A.L. and Rubin, J. 1987. A collection of papers discussing research that demonstrate that second language learners bring a varied range of learning skills to the task of acquiring second language competence.

Whitney, N. 1983 and 1985. A two-part course for secondary students at pre-intermediate level containing training in how to learn English and a progress check for students and teachers at the end of each unit.

# Stage 1 Preparation for language learning

## 1.1 What do you expect from your course?

| Materials: | Learner's Book page 5 |
|---|---|
| | Cassette |
| | Prepared overhead projector transparency / board |
| Items to cover: | Discussion arising from the questions should cover language learning, accuracy and fluency, course aims and methodology, the role of the teacher and an introduction to learner training. |
| Time: | 30–45 minutes |

This section is designed to be used at the beginning of a new course, after the learners have finished 'getting to know each other' activities.

As teacher, you have the key role. It is your task to encourage the learners to give their opinions and talk about their experiences in a stress-free atmosphere so that they can gain the maximum benefit from this session.

It is anticipated that learners at an intermediate level will be able to discuss the questions in English — with help from you, if necessary — but we see no reason why the mother tongue or a common language should not be used if this is more practicable.

1.  Ask the learners to discuss the questions in pairs for 10–15 minutes. If your learners are young, or come from backgrounds where it is unusual for them to be asked to give personal opinions, they may find this difficult. In this case, you could play the recordings of other learners giving their opinions and use these as a basis for discussion in your group. Ask if your learners feel the same way as any of the recorded learners and why.

    Alternatively, if your class is more confident, you could play the recording *after* the initial discussion.

2. Initiate a class discussion covering each question.
   a) Do you think you are good at learning languages? Why or why not?
      This question provides an opportunity for learners to talk about
      themselves as language learners. It may be that past learning
      experiences have led them to form negative views about themselves
      or about English. Encourage learners to express any opinions or
      doubts that they have and try to be supportive.

      The question 'What is a "good language learner"?' may arise
      here. There appear to be no right or wrong ways of learning –
      only what works for each individual. We suggest you emphasise to
      your learners the benefits of being willing to experiment with differ-
      ent ways of learning and of keeping an open mind about the vari-
      ous activities they will be encouraged to try in this book and during
      their course.

      **Tapescript:**

      *Interviewer:* Do you think you are good at learning languages?
      *Maria Elena (Colombia):* No, I no think I'm very good at learning lan-
        guages.
      *Interviewer:* Why not?
      *Maria Elena:* Um . . . I find quite difficult er . . . speaking.

      *Ana (Spain):* Er . . . well, I . . . I don't think I'm bad at languages I think
        er . . . I don't have great difficulties in learning languages or picking up
        languages. Um . . . I don't know whether it is because I . . . I like them,
        I'm really motivated and I am enjoy it.

      *Interviewer:* Do you think you are good at learning languages?
      *Beliyou (Ethiopia):* Um . . . I think I'm all right.
      *Interviewer:* Why's that?
      *Beliyou:* Um . . . because I'm interested in languages and I think
        I . . . I . . . I . . . listen carefully. I don't know, I mean, I don't know if
        I'm fluent, but I . . . I think I can er I can imitate sounds.

      *Fumiko (Japan):* Yes, I think so, that's why I can talk with you now but um
        I think maybe why I am a good learner is mainly I'm very interested in
        talking with other people, not not only English, but with Japanese. I'm
        very talkative.

      *Kate (England):* I think I'm probably better than average, yes, actually
        because I am genuinely interested in learning languages and I tend not to
        mind making a fool of myself, as it were. I don't mind taking risks when
        I'm at the learning stage and even, like, now I consider myself to be very
        rusty speaking, say, French or German, I don't actually mind using the
        language and I think my ears do pick up other things that I will then later
        use and so on.

      *Interviewer:* Jim, do you think you are good at learning er . . . languages?
      *Jim (England):* No, I'm afraid I don't think I am.
      *Interviewer:* Why not?

*Jim:* Um . . . Because I think um . . . you have to be in the country concerned to really learn a language and I haven't travelled very much abroad, and just to learn from books I find very difficult.

*Interviewer:* Coovi, do you think you are good at learning languages?
*Coovi (Benin):* Yes, I am.
*Interviewer:* How many do you speak?
*Coovi:* I speak at least eight languages and er four dialects. Yes. African dialects, you see. Er . . . I speak, I can speak English, French, Spanish, Mina, Ewe, Yoruba, Adja and er I can speak, as I said, four other dialects, like Gbesin, Aizo, Kotafon and er Dendi, some Dendi. Yes, I think I can . . . I'm very er er I'm not er I think I can master those languages. I've mastered them very well because you have to speak those languages because there are many tribes in Benin and er in er two kilometres . . . in two miles . . . you meet other people and you have to speak their language, you have to go by and that's why, if you are Beninois, you are almost compelled to know those languages . . . and that's why I could speak those languages. Yes.

b) What do you think is the best way to learn a new language? Why? The response is likely to be, 'By living in the country where they speak that language because you are forced to speak it too.' Do all your learners agree?

Ask: 'Is it necessary to attend a language course before or as well as your visit?' You will probably finish with some division of opinion. At this point, you can mention that everybody has different learning styles, preferences and needs. This provides a lead-in for discussion of the next question, during which you can explain the methodology, aims, etc. of your course.

**Tapescript:**

*Interviewer:* What do you think is the best way to learn a new language?
*Maria Elena (Colombia):* OK I think . . . it um it . . . depends on the person, but for me, I think it's just practising. Er I mean, I need a person who I could talk to . . . so . . . again, in Colombia it's quite difficult to practise because we are a monolingual country, so we have very few opportunity to to speak, you know, to practise with different people.

*Ann (Eire):* Well, I suppose it's different for different people. I like to hear the sounds first, but then I like to see them written down. If I don't see the words written, then I don't remember them.

*Paz (Spain):* I think the best way to learn a language is to go to the country where they speak the language.

*Beliyou (Ethiopia):* Well, the best way would be to live among the speakers of the language and speak it, practise it there, I mean, not formally, but just informally, without knowing it.

*Fumiko (Japan):* I think the best way, er from my experience maybe, to have a boyfriend.

*Yuen (Hong Kong):* I think the best way to learn English is forget about
  your mother tongue and then don't translate − that's the main point.
*Kate (England):* I er . . . I don't think there is a best way. For me,
  personally, I think it's probably to have some formal learning but also a
  great deal of living in the country where the language is spoken and
  preferably continually for at least a few weeks surrounded by it and then
  I tend to sort of put the two things together − my f . . . formal learning
  plus what I'm hearing around me or seeing . . . on posters, listening to
  the radio, things like that. So, I guess, for me, it's a mixture, and that's
  probably what I would recommend to most people.

*Interviewer:* What do you think is the best way then to learn a foreign
  language?
*Jim (England):* I think probably the best way is to learn like you learn your
  mother tongue, which is to be immersed in the country and the language
  and then come to grips with the grammar and the structure of the
  language later, once you can communicate.

c) What kinds of activities do you think should be included in your
   course? Why?
   Ask learners for their opinions about this. You could then go on to
   explain that we can divide language learning into two types:
   i)   formal learning (conscious learning)
   ii)  picking up (subconscious acquisition).
   You could put the following diagram on the board or overhead
   projector. Explain what the two types involve and point out that
   both may take place either in or outside the classroom.

**Formal language learning**

(thinking consciously about
the language)

e.g. doing a grammar exercise or
   practising pronunciation
   – in the classroom
   – at home
   – in the self-access centre

Main focus on *accuracy*

**Picking up language**

(learning a language without
thinking consciously about it)

e.g. watching a film or listening
   to a conversation
   – in the classroom
   – at home
   – at the cinema

Main focus on *fluency*

Effective
language
user

Make the point that learners may prefer or be better at one type of learning, but that, in order to be an effective all-round user of the language, they need practice in both.

Move on to explain how your course takes into account both types of learning. (The balance between the two may depend, for example, on whether or not the course is being held in an English-speaking country where learners get additional exposure to the target language outside the classroom.) Introduce the idea that for activities which involve formal learning *accuracy* is important, while for activities where communication is the main focus, *fluency* is more important. Talk about your course timetable and the types of activity learners will be asked to participate in, relating these to accuracy or fluency practice, like this:

| *Accuracy* | *Fluency* |
|---|---|
| pronunciation practice | discussions |
| grammar exercises | group work / pair work |
| language laboratory drills | role plays |
| etc. | etc. |

State your normal procedures for correcting mistakes during such activities: *immediately* during accuracy work and *after* fluency work. If learners understand these distinctions from the beginning of the course there should be no confusion or mismatch of expectations. Tell your learners that the teacher(s) will always try to make it clear whether an activity focusses on accuracy or fluency or both, so that they know what they are practising and why. It is obviously very important that the teacher(s) should be consistent about this throughout the course.

The preceding explanations might seem rather detailed at first glance, but they are, nevertheless, vital both for the relationship between learners and teacher(s) and for the smooth running of the learner training programme and your course.

You can then tell your learners that they have just experienced their first session of *learner training*, that is helping them learn how to learn. Spend a few minutes explaining to the learners what learner training is (see page 2), how it is to be incorporated into their course and the role that the Learner's Book will play in it. This is also the appropriate time to make learners aware of your role during their learner training programme and their language course. Take learners through the Introduction in the Learner's Book and allow them time to familiarise themselves with the layout of the book.

**Further reading**

Altman, H.B. and James, C.V. (eds.) 1980. (See page 34.)
Crookall, D. 1983. (See page 34.)
Dulay, H. et al. 1982. A text on second language acquisition presenting the latest research in the field.
Krashen, S. 1981. (See page 35.)
Naiman, N. et al. 1978. (See page 35.)
Norrish, J. 1983. A review of the current thinking on errors in language learning.
Rubin, J. 1975. (See page 36.)
Rubin, J. and Thompson, I. 1982. (See page 36.)
Stern, H.H. 1975. (See page 36.)
Wenden, A.L. 1986a. (See page 37.)

# 1.2 What sort of language learner are you?

| | |
|---|---|
| Materials: | Learner's Book pages 6–9 |
| Items to cover: | Quiz: different learning styles, suggestions for becoming a more effective language learner. |
| Time: | 10–15 minutes |

We recommend that this quiz should directly follow *1.1 What do you expect from your course?* if it is to be done in class. It could also be done as homework, but it is then useful to have a follow-up class discussion so that learners hear about each other's 'results' and can express their opinions and ask questions.

Learning styles or habits may be a product of the learner's personality, cultural background, past learning experience and training; they may also be influenced by the task he or she is engaged in at present. Learning styles may therefore be innate or acquired. Teachers can accommodate the variety of learning styles in their classes by presenting new language in different ways, providing the opportunity for group or pair work in addition to individual work, providing opportunities for learners to make choices about what they learn and how they learn and by using a wide selection of learning materials. However, the learners themselves are rarely asked to reflect on what sort of language learners they think they are.

The aim of this activity is to help learners become aware of the fact that:

a) different learning styles exist
b) each learner has his or her own learning style or habits
c) it is possible that because of these particular learning styles or habits, the learner may be neglecting other learning strategies which could help him or her become a more effective language learner.

The quiz in the Learner's Book provides the *starting point* for learners to begin the process of reflection on their personal learning styles and habits and the implications of these for their language learning. This means that when they move on to the activities in Stage 2, they should be in a better position to consider the effectiveness of various learning strategies.

The quiz and the comments provide a greatly simplified representation of Krashen's (1981) distinction between conscious learning and subconscious acquisition and reflect these two extremes:

*conscious* _____ *subconscious*
*learning*                                              *acquisition*

as well as Kolb's (1984) view of comprehension and apprehension.

We have chosen to use the above very broad division, as we have found that it is one which learners can readily understand and apply to themselves. We have not included the terms 'conscious learning' and 'subconscious acquisition' in the Learner's Book but you may wish to introduce these if you think your learners would be interested. Many are.

We do not intend this activity to suggest to learners that they each have only one learning style, since there are so many variables which affect the choice of learning strategy at any particular time. Nor do we feel it would be useful to analyse learning styles in greater detail, since this would entail giving learners time-consuming banks of questions to answer. Furthermore, the interpretation of the results might prove too sophisticated a task for learners. In our experience, too, giving learners a precise 'label' related to a particular learning style tends to stop them from actively evaluating their own learning as they learn.

The learner who tends towards conscious learning, we have called *Analytic?* and the learner who tends towards subconscious acquisition, we have called *Relaxed?* Many learners, however, do not fall neatly into either of these two categories; for the sake of simplicity, we have called them *A mixture?* In addition, we have included a category called *Not sure?* for those learners who may never have considered what sort of learner they are and who find it difficult to answer the questions in the quiz. More detailed notes on these categories follow.

Check that the learners understand the questions in the quiz; ask them to answer individually and calculate their score. They should then read the appropriate comments. Each set of comments is linked to some suggestions to help the learners become aware of strategies they might be neglecting, which might help them become more effective language learners. None of the comments are meant to be negative. All learning styles may be successful sometimes, just as all may bring problems with them. Lead a group discussion about the learners' 'results' and their possible implications for learning during the course.

### Analytic?

This type of learner may be obsessed with being accurate. The Suggestions outline various ways of improving fluency.

### Relaxed?

This type of learner may generally be quite fluent, but not always very accurate. The Suggestions encourage such learners to become more consciously involved in their learning and to consider various ways of improving accuracy.

### A mixture?

This type of learner does not fall neatly into either of the preceding categories. The Suggestion encourages such learners to look at the descriptions for *Analytic?* and *Relaxed?*, try to decide which one they are closer to and to identify areas of learning that may perhaps be worked on.

### Not sure?

This type of learner may never have reflected on him or herself as a language learner before and may find it difficult to give definite answers to the questions in the quiz at this stage. The Suggestion encourages such learners to read the descriptions for *Analytic?* and *Relaxed?* and to use these as a basis for trying to become more aware of their learning during the course.

We suggest that learners do this quiz again later in the course and compare results.

---

**Further reading**

Ellis, G. and Sinclair, B. forthcoming. This paper considers the issue of learning styles from the point of view of the practising teacher and the foreign language learner.

Entwistle, N.J. and Ramsden, P. 1983. An abridged version of the final report on a five-year Social Science Research Council research programme begun in 1976, which investigated students' approaches to learning in order to determine the extent to which these reflected the effects of teaching and assessment demands rather than representing relatively stable characteristics of the individual learner.

Flinders, S. 1984. This article argues that an understanding of the language learner's learning profile is an important prerequisite to the implementation of a course programme. The author discusses the difficulties of introducing case studies to students who are recent products of the French secondary school system and argues that, once the students accept this new approach to learning, they make good progress.

Kolb, D. A. 1984. This book provides a comprehensive and systematic statement of the theory of experiential learning, and proposes a model which forms a typology of individual learning styles and structures of knowledge in different academic disciplines and professions. It also includes a theory of adult development.

Krashen, S. 1981. (See page 35.)

McConnell, J. 1981. This article argues that particular professional groups develop their own patterns of thought as a result of their professional training, and that these patterns will determine their language learning strategies.

Narcy, J.P. 1983. This article describes a study at an Institut Universitaire de Technologie in France. It identifies learning styles and uses these findings to help the teacher select appropriate classroom techniques and activities.

O'Malley, J.M. et al. 1985a. (See page 36.)

O'Malley, J.M. et al. 1985b. (See page 36.)

Reiss, M.A. 1983. A review of the literature on variables in language learning such as personality, cognitive styles, language learning strategies and techniques, and individual learning styles and techniques. It concludes with ten suggestions to enable the language teacher to help poor language learners.

Skehan, P. forthcoming. (See page 36.)

Whitling, D. 1982. An article written for the language learner about recent developments in language learning theory, namely, Krashen's Monitor Theory.

# 1.3  Why do you need or want to learn English?

| Materials: | Learner's Book pages 10–11<br>Cassette |
|---|---|
| Items to cover: | 1. Analysing your needs<br>2. Prioritising your needs |
| Time: | 20 minutes |

It is normal practice in many language schools to issue potential students with a ready-printed, detailed questionnaire in order to establish their language needs. This questionnaire is usually designed by the institution; it often consists of Yes/No questions or boxes to tick, etc., and its main aim is to inform the course planner about the learners and to aid course design. The needs analysis in this learner training programme attempts to be more learner-centred, in that it is the learners who describe their language needs, selecting not from a teacher's list, but from their own experience.

Here, the learners are asked to think about their needs in terms that are relatively easy for them. In our experience, they often describe their needs in rather imprecise ways: for example, 'I want to improve my speaking' or 'I need more grammar'. We do not believe it to be desirable to go into further detail at this stage since we have found that it can be unrealistic to expect learners at the beginning of their course to be able to perform a very detailed needs analysis of their own. However, later on in Stage 2, learners are trained to set themselves more detailed and realistic short-term aims.

## 1  Analysing your needs

Refer your learners to the Learner's Book for an example of how to do a needs analysis. The cassette provides examples of learners talking about their reasons for learning English and may be used to introduce your learners to the topic and to start them thinking. Ask your learners to do their own needs analysis and offer guidance and advice, where necessary.

**Tapescript**

*Interviewer:* Why do you need or want to learn English?

*Maria Elena (Colombia):* Er . . . I think it's because er we have very few English teachers. Um I would like to be a teacher. If . . . My mother is a teacher and I think I i . . . i also . . . that encouraged me to carry on with this profession.

*Ana (Spain):* Um, well, there are a few reasons. O . . . Originally, my my er, my first aim was to complement my my studies. I I'd done um . . . History of Art at the university and I er thought I could sort of become um, I . . . like a tourist guide or um sort of work in tourism and er I thought that, with Art and languages, that'd be the perfect mixture, but, eventually, I thought it was a boring profession anyway.

*Beliyou (Ethiopia):* Er, well um the whole world operates in English mostly and er it's very important in in Ethiopia — right, everybody has to do it.

*Paz (Spain):* Er . . . because . . . um . . . when . . . when I . . . when I learnt English it was . . . er . . . when I was 17 . . . it was because I was very, very, very interested on er . . . on English er . . . culture.

*Chen (China):* Well, I'm afraid I'm no good at mathematics and chemistry and physics and I would love to go to university. So, my only choice — either to take Chinese as my subject or English and I thought, there are a lot of people who take Chinese so English might be well, maybe easier for me to get a chance to go to university. That's all.

*Yuen (Hong Kong):* I'm studying in England, so I have to speak English.

*Marisol (Spain):* Er I am learning English because I think is er . . . an important language in the world . . . um because you can . . . um . . . commun . . . communicate er everything you need not only in your country, in all the countries. Is very important.

## 2 Prioritising your needs

Learners are asked to complete an initial self-assessment, that is 'Where am I now?' so they are in a better position to prioritise their needs. Ask them to look at Stig's example and then complete their own self-assessment and prioritise their needs. Let them decide which number to circle on their personal self-assessment scale.

These activities will give learners a clearer picture of which skills they need to concentrate on in Stage 2. If you have a class of learners with different learning priorities, you may need to negotiate with them how Stage 2 will be covered, for example, by:

— reaching a compromise with the class about which skills to cover and in which order
— having individuals or groups work separately.

Whether and how you do this will depend, of course, on your particular teaching context and on the nature of the course and its syllabus.

---

**Further reading**

Allwright, R.L. 1982. This paper describes an approach to help Polish research scientists on two three-week residential courses perceive and pursue their needs.
Oskarsson, M. 1980. (See page 78.)
Richterich, R. and Chancerel, J.L. 1980. Papers from the Council of Europe project on a unit credit system for modern language learning by adults, now the Modern Languages Project. Discusses the concept of learners' needs and expands this to cover aspects of the personal and social development of the individual.
Rivers, W.M. 1983. (See page 36.) See chapter 10.

# 1.4 How do you organise your learning?

| | |
|---|---|
| Materials: | Learner's Book pages 12–17<br>Selection of dictionaries<br>Selection of grammar books<br>Information about language learning resources in your school<br>Copies of viewing guides, listening guides e.g. *London Calling, BBC English by Radio and TV*, entertainment guides<br>Information about libraries, book shops, etc. in your area |
| Items to cover: | *1. Have you got a dictionary?*<br>Selecting a suitable dictionary.<br>*2. Have you got a grammar book?*<br>Selecting a suitable grammar book.<br>*3. What other resources have you got?*<br>Radio, television, cinema, shops, clubs, etc.<br>*4. How do you organise your materials?*<br>*5. How much time have you got to learn English?*<br>*6. How do you organise your time?*<br>Planning review sessions. |
| Time: | Flexible: some of the activities could be done in class or individually by learners. We do not recommend discussing all the activities in class in one session. |

## 1 Have you got a dictionary?

Learners often have inadequate dictionary facilities. For example, they may be using small, out-of-date bilingual dictionaries and may not have considered the potential of alternatives, e.g. monolingual, illustrated, active study dictionaries. The chart included in the Learner's Book encourages them to consider useful criteria other than size and price.

Ask your learners to bring in their own dictionaries. If possible, bring in a selection yourself, which you recommend for learners, including examples of monolingual and more recently published dictionaries.

You might also wish to draw your learners' attention to the various workbooks and sections in study skills books which train students to use their dictionaries effectively (see *Recommended for learners*).

After the survey, encourage your learners to reconsider the dictionary facilities available to them. Give advice and guidance where necessary.

## 2   Have you got a grammar book?

Learners may have outdated grammar books which do not take account of the recent changes in language use. Explanations may be complicated, obscure and difficult to understand. Conversely, they may be over-simplified and therefore not tell the truth. The chart in the Learner's Book encourages learners to be more critical of the grammar books available to them. Ask them to bring their own grammar books to class as well as providing a selection yourself if possible.

## 3   What other resources have you got?

Direct the learners to the list of resources in the Learner's Book and encourage them to find out about the ones they are interested in. Be prepared to give information and advice where necessary about resources available in your institution and locally.

## 4   How do you organise your materials?

Ask learners to read the suggestions provided and encourage a further exchange of ideas. You could encourage them to create class libraries as well as Personal language banks.

## 5   How much time have you got to learn English?

We suggest learners complete the chart in the Learner's Book, which is adapted from Holec (1981:35–7), to encourage them to be realistic about the time they have available for their language learning. This could be done as a pairwork activity which would provide further language practice. For example, Learner A would ask Learner B, 'How much time do you spend sleeping in a typical week?'

## 6   How do you organise your time?

There is evidence to show that in order to transfer items being learnt from short-term memory to long-term memory, reviewing should be done at specific intervals (see graphs on page 17). Encourage your learners to apply these findings to their own language learning.

**Further reading**

Buzan, T. 1982. This book explains how study can become more effective, problems can be solved more readily and ways of thinking can be developed.

Hedge, T. 1985b. A guide for the teacher on the selection and use of graded readers. Chapter 5 considers the practical issues involved in setting up a class library to encourage extensive reading.

Marshall, L.A. and Rowland, F. 1983. (See page 35.)

Palmer, R. and Pope, C. 1984. This book offers an approach to effective study for students at home or at college, by helping them find and adopt the study methods most suited to their needs.

Rubin, J. and Thompson, I. 1982. (See page 36.)

Stevick, E.W. 1976. An exploration of the language learning process.

*Recommended for learners*

Davies, E. and Whitney, N. 1984. See Section 1. (See page 78.)

Eastwood, J. and Mackin, R. 1982. A reference book for students of EFL covering grammatical structures and communicative functions that are generally taught in the first three or four years of English.

Jones, C. 1985. A do-it-yourself dictionary-building computer database program.

Murphy, R. 1985. This book combines reference grammar and practice exercises. For self-study or classroom use.

Swan, M. 1980. A reference grammar for intermediate to advanced students of English and their teachers.

Underhill, A. 1980. A practice book for users of the Oxford Advanced Learner's Dictionary of Current English to enable them to become effective dictionary users. Activities cover all aspects of dictionary use.

# 1.5 How motivated are you?

| Materials: | Learner's Book pages 18–19<br>Graph paper (optional) |
|---|---|
| Items to cover: | How motivation can affect learning, how to keep a motivation graph. |
| Time: | 10 minutes |

a) Ask your learners to look at Geraldine's motivation graph and her comments on her high and low points.

b) Ask the learners to consider what factors might affect their motivation during their course. How do they feel now? Why? How did they feel yesterday? Why?

   You might like to give them graph paper and encourage them to produce their own motivation graphs, or they could use the graph in the Learner's Book. You could suggest that they bring these graphs into class in order to compare stages of motivation and the reasons for these.

**Further reading**

Alatis, J.E. 1976. This paper argues that teachers should encourage their students, as well as the general public, to feel motivated to learn a second language.

Allwright, R.L. 1977. This article considers the teacher's responsibility for motivating his or her learners by outlining potential sources of and different sorts of motivation.

Burstall, C. 1975. This paper examines the influence of motivational factors on foreign language learning and considers 'integrative' versus 'instrumental' motivation, the effect of contact with the foreign culture, the influence of socio-economic factors, sex differences in foreign language learning, achievement in the small school, teacher-pupil interaction and the effect on the pupil of different methods of presenting foreign language material. It also considers the evidence for the existence of an 'optimum age' for foreign language learning.

Gardner, R.C. and Lambert, W.E. 1972. This book summarises research into how some people can learn a foreign language more quickly and expertly than others. It focusses on individual differences in skill using foreign languages.

Holden, S. 1983. Papers from the 1983 Bologna Conference. Chapter 2 contains four papers dealing with motivation of the learner.
Littlejohn, A. 1985. (See page 35.)
Porter Ladousse, G. 1982. (See page 36.)
Skehan, P. forthcoming. (See page 36.)
Stern, H.H. 1983. (See page 36.) See chapter 17.

# 1.6 What can you do in a self-access centre*?

| Materials: | Learner's Book pages 20–23<br>Cassette<br>Information material about your self-access centre |
|---|---|
| Items to cover: | 1. *In class*<br>What does 'self-access' mean? Facilities and organisation of the self-access centre in your school, the purposes of a self-access centre, the advantages and disadvantages of using a self-access centre.<br>2. *In the self-access centre*<br>Finding out how to use the self-access centre.<br>3. *Time to experiment*<br>Trying out the self-access centre.<br>4. *One learner's experience*<br>5. *Keeping records* |
| Time: | 90 minutes–2 hours |

Self-access centres can vary considerably from school to school and may range from a cardboard box with materials in it to a complex centre managed by librarian staff with every conceivable type of hardware and software. Some schools encourage very directed 'self-study' with the use of the self-access centre timetabled into a course or with a teacher setting learning tasks for individuals – or perhaps a mixture of both. Other schools may leave the frequency and type of use of the self-access centre entirely up to the learner. Whatever system your school employs, however, it is more than likely that the learners will need a considerable amount of familiarisation and training before they are able to understand fully the potential of the self-access centre and begin to make the best use of it.

At English International, a school in Lyons, France, which encourages its learners to use the self-access centre as often as possible, it has been found that, in general, it takes a new learner approximately 30 hours of

* Your school may have a different name for it.

self-access learning before he or she becomes proficient in maximising the resources and recognising the strategies which are most successful for him or her. On short, intensive courses, for example, it may not be possible or desirable to spend a lot of time inducting learners into the use of the self-access centre; in this case we recommend the activities in this section be used in the classroom as well as in the self-access centre.

There are three basic problems that we may encounter when we try to encourage learners to use a self-access centre. Firstly, there is the learner whose past learning experiences have provided him or her with little or no opportunity for taking on responsibility for his or her own learning. These learners may be teacher-dependent and feel insecure and very uncomfortable, perhaps even cheated, if they are suddenly expected to work alone and make choices about how and with what materials they will learn. Secondly, learners worry about the apparent wasting of time that happens when they go into a self-access centre on the first few occasions — especially if they are paying fees for what they think should be a highly organised or perhaps intensive course. They can very quickly lose motivation if they do not experience immediate success with a self-study task. Thirdly, we encounter opposition simply because the learner really does not like to learn in this way or is not in the mood for experimentation. We believe that all these problems can be tackled by a systematic induction.

## 1  In class

Your learners may have different levels of awareness regarding the use of a self-access centre. This activity will enable you to assess these. Ask your learners to consider the points in the Learner's Book in pairs and then lead a class discussion.

a) and (b) This is a chance for the learners to exchange information, but keep it brief.

c) Your learners may not come up with many ideas at this stage. If the purposes listed here do not arise from the discussion, suggest them yourself and ask the learners to consider their importance:

*to give the opportunity for self-study*
- to work without a teacher, either alone or with other learners
- to follow up individual interests
- to work on specific individual language problems
- to provide opportunity for study outside class time

*to develop learner autonomy*
- to practise making critical decisions regarding materials and activities

   – to experiment with different learning or practice activities
   – to discover learning strategies which suit learners personally
   – to practise assessing learning and monitoring progress

*to save the school money and effort*
Some learners, especially those who feel they have paid a lot for a
course, may see the self-access centre as a way of saving on teacher
time, lesson preparation, etc. It is worth bringing this idea into the
open so that you can reassure learners that the self-access centre is
primarily for *their* benefit.

d)   This recycles some of the ideas from (c) and should act as reinforce-
     ment. Some learners may wish to mention more specific personal
     advantages, such as, 'I'll be able to look again at difficult grammar
     points we did in class. I find I can't always concentrate in class.'
        The disadvantages may be very personal and may include:
     – I wouldn't know what to do (I need a teacher).
     – I wouldn't know if the materials were right for me.
     – How would I know if I were correct or making too many mistakes?
     – I can only improve if I am corrected by the teacher.
     – I hate working alone.
     – I get bored quickly.
     – I have no time for extra study.
     It can be very difficult to discourage such negative feelings without
     giving the learners the opportunity to experiment with learning in a
     self-access centre. At this point, encourage your learners to *try* it and
     then see whether their worries are justified. You may like to remind
     them of the benefits of experimenting with different learning
     techniques. The next two activities should help to reassure them.

## 2   In the self-access centre

This activity encourages information gathering and sharing; learners
could usefully work in pairs. Allow approximately ten minutes for
research in the centre. If learners wish to spend more time in there, they
can return later. By the end of the class feedback session, your class
should know the basic organisation and operating mode(s) of your self-
access centre. If your centre has learner information leaflets, etc. make
sure everybody gets a copy.

## 3   Time to experiment

This activity allows learners to experiment with using the self-access
centre and to test their hypotheses about doing so.
   This is a particularly useful activity for teachers to try, too, as it is not

until one has tried working in a self-access centre that one can really be aware of its potential. We suggest you try the following as an in-service teacher training activity in your school, using the same discussion points as in the Learner's Book.

Assemble a range of materials which could be used for self-study in a particular language or several different languages, e.g. German, French, Spanish. Group the materials first of all according to language, and then according to material types (e.g. reading materials, cassettes).

Participants select a language that they know something of (it could be literally only a few words) and then choose materials or activities to work on for approximately 40–45 minutes. The group should then come together to discuss the points in the Learner's Book.

This activity can be repeated regularly with teachers (or trainee teachers) with the participants varying the language, so that, for example, one time they would choose a language they were proficient in and another time a language where they knew only a very little. In this way, teachers can become more aware of the problems facing learners at different levels in a self-access centre.

With your learners, you will probably find that doing this activity once only will not be particularly productive. We recommend that a regular time is set aside for discussing self-access work, so that learners experience and hear about a wide range of strategies, and opinions.

## 4   One learner's experience

The cassette gives an expanded and more detailed version of the experiences of Pierre, a French learner, in the self-access centre. You may decide to use it as a stimulus for your learners' discussion, as a listening exercise in its own right, or as reinforcement after the discussion. Learners could, for example, look in the Learner's Book and make predictions as to what Pierre says next, or they may make notes and compare Pierre's experiences with their own. This recording may also be placed in the self-access centre for learners to use.

**Tapescript**

i) I always seem to have problems when I listen to English, so I decided to listen to a cassette in the self-access centre. I didn't know what kind of cassette, but I thought maybe something like a news broadcast.

ii) When I got in there, I had a look at the cassettes and found one of the day before yesterday's news. I thought it wouldn't be too difficult because I had looked at a newspaper yesterday and we had discussed the news in class too.

   After a couple of minutes, though, I got bored, so I decided to look for something else to do. A friend of mine was looking at a magazine, so I went over for a look. I looked through a couple of magazines,

c

thinking I would find an article to read. Actually, I just looked at some cartoons and the pictures. Then, in one of the magazines there was a short article about what to look for when buying a new bicycle. I am thinking of doing that because I'd like to get out and about more in the countryside while I'm here. So, anyway, I thought I would have a look.

iii)   First, I read the whole article as quickly as I could – just to get the main ideas. There were a lot of words to do with parts of the bicycle that I didn't know, so I decided to concentrate on them next. There was also a picture of a bicycle with its parts labelled, so I looked at this and tried to remember the words. I wrote a list of the tricky ones with a translation. Then, I used my list to test myself. I read the article again and when I came to one of those words that I couldn't remember straight away, I stopped and tried to guess. Then I checked the picture to see if I was right. I thought it was quite easy to remember the words as I read. When I thought I knew all the parts of the bicycle, I read the article again and made a list of all the tips it gave for buying a new bicycle; it took me about 20 minutes in all.

iv)   Generally, I think my strategy was good, but I found I didn't really need the list of words and their translations that I had made. I think a diagram of a bicycle with labels might be more useful, but I don't think I'll forget the words, anyway.

     Perhaps it would be a good idea for me to make a diagram myself tonight, as a kind of test.

v)    The only problem I had was that my friend kept trying to talk to me and I don't like being interrupted when I'm concentrating.

vi)   I enjoyed using the self-access centre, though it took a while for me to find something to do.

## 5   Keeping records

Your school probably has its own method of keeping records of work done by students (student record cards, notebooks, etc.). Explain to the learners that this is only *one* suggestion and that there are many different ways of doing this (see Learner's Book page 24 for an illustration).

    Some learners may not wish to keep personal records at all. In this case we recommend explaining the advantages of doing so, but leaving the final decision to the learner.

---

**Further reading**

Crookall, D. 1985. This article describes an extensive reading exercise. Guidelines are provided on how to make a student reading package for self-access work, as well as suggestions for its use in the classroom.

Dickinson, L. 1981. A discussion of issues involved in self-access learning, such as preparation of the learner, needs analysis, materials and administrative considerations.

Ely, P. 1985. This book presents 22 different language laboratory ideas and activities involving accurate listening, accurate communication between students and activities where the student provides appropriate and spontaneous responses to a series of stimuli.

Harding-Esch, E. 1982. An outline of some of the pedagogical and administrative problems involved in the organisation and development of an open-access and video library.

Riley, P. 1986. This article clarifies some of the issues involved in running a self-access system by examining the roles of the main participants, for example, technician, helper, librarian-secretary, learner. It also includes a glossary of terms which occur frequently in discussion on language learning schemes where some kind of effort is made to focus on the learner.

Windeatt, S. 1980. A paper which describes a project in self-access learning at Lancaster University for overseas in-sessional students.

# Stage 2   Skills training

## 2.1   Extending vocabulary

─────── ■ ☐ ☐ ☐ ☐ ☐ ───────────────

## Step 1   How do you feel about learning vocabulary?

| | |
|---|---|
| Materials: | Learner's Book page 27 |
| Items to cover: | Learners' attitudes towards vocabulary can affect the way they learn. |
| Time: | 15 minutes |

1. Ask your learners to consider the attitudes represented by Brigitte and Adel; both have negative and positive aspects. Lead a class discussion and elicit or suggest the following points:

### Brigitte

*Possible positive points*
- enthusiastic
- motivated
- desire to be clear and precise
- aspiration to use the language in a rich and varied way and to be able to cope in all situations
- has an efficient system for learning vocabulary

*Possible negative points*
- not enough selection, tries to learn everything and may therefore not always be successful
- spends too much time on developing vocabulary to the the detriment of other skills

### Adel

*Possible positive points*
- shows awareness of various communication strategies e.g. paraphrasing, paralinguistics

*Possible negative points*
- may not be able to express himself adequately
- may lead to boring, repetitive, verbose style

—adventuresome, risk-taking approach, e.g. inventing new words and experimenting

— lack of vocabulary may also affect performance in other skills, e.g. comprehension
— difficult for him to feel he is making any significant progress — can be demotivating

2. and 3. Ask your learners to think about their own attitudes towards learning English vocabulary and to discuss these in class. Encourage them to consider what effect these attitudes may have on their vocabulary learning.

■ ■ □ □ □ □ □

# Step 2    What do you know about English vocabulary?

| Materials: | Learner's Book pages 28–29 |
|---|---|
| Items to cover: | *1. Active and passive vocabulary*<br>*2. Knowing a word* |
| Time: | 15–20 minutes |

## 1   Active and passive vocabulary

Passive vocabulary refers to language items that can be *recognised and understood* in the context of reading or listening, and active vocabulary to items which the learner can *use appropriately* in speaking or writing. Sidsel expresses the anxiety felt by many learners about their lack of active vocabulary. Often they are not aware of the distinction between active and passive vocabulary, nor of the fact that it is usual to have a far larger passive vocabulary than an active one. Indeed, many are not aware that this is usual for a native speaker too.

Ask learners to complete (a) and (b) in pairs.

**Answers**

a) Estimates of the passive vocabulary of educated native speakers of English vary widely. They range between 50,000 and 250,000 words and include words derived from the same root, e.g. advise, adviser, advisory.

b) Approximately 10,000.

In most cases, people underestimate the number of words. This information is not meant to be daunting, but enlightening. Emphasise that it is usual to understand more than you can say. This can lead into a class discussion of (c).

## 2  Knowing a word

a) Go through the points, eliciting or giving examples; those included here are only suggestions and you will probably have your own which are more relevant to your learners. The list is adapted from Wallace (1982:27).

| *Point* | *Example* |
|---|---|
| i) to understand it when it is written and/or spoken | |
| ii) to recall it when you need it | |
| iii) to use it with the correct meaning | not calling a table a 'chair' |
| iv) to use it in a grammatically correct way | 'She sang very well' (*not* 'She sang very good') |
| v) to pronounce it correctly (i.e. with an acceptable pronunciation) | Discuss what 'acceptable' means with regard to pronunciation. |
| vi) to know which other words you can use with it | 'a beautiful view' (*not* 'a good looking view'); 'an interesting table' (*not* 'an exciting table'); 'fish and chips' (*not* 'chips and fish'); 'black and white' (*not* 'white and black') |
| vii) to spell it correctly | Spelling can alter meaning: 'weight' or 'wait'? 'poor' or 'pour'? 'sore' or 'saw'? 'draught' or 'draft'? |

| viii) to use it in the right situation (i.e. appropriacy) | 'Mrs Thatcher, would you like to take a seat?' (*not* 'Mrs Thatcher, would you like to park your bum here?') |
|---|---|
| ix)  to know if it has positive or negative associations (i.e. connotations) | 'He's a bachelor, she's a spinster.'* Explain the positive connotations of 'bachelor' and the negative connotations of 'spinster' in the minds of many native speakers of English. |

\* bachelor = desirable, attractive, virile
  spinster = undesirable, unattractive, dull, frigid

b) Further reference will be made to this in Step 3(1).

c) Encourage an exchange of ideas here.

d) Ask your learners to consider what kinds of words would be most useful for them to learn and why. Make suggestions as to where they could find these words, for example specialised dictionaries, magazines, books, newspapers, course books.

───── ■■■□□□ ─────

# Step 3   How well are you doing?

| Materials: | Learner's Book pages 30–32 |
|---|---|
| Items to cover: | *Introduction* <br> *1. Points to assess* <br> *2. Test yourself in a practice activity* <br> *3. Assess your performance in a real-life situation* <br> *4. Examples* |
| Time: | 15–20 minutes when you introduce self-assessment in this skill for the first time. Thereafter, 5–10 minute sessions when necessary. |

## Introduction

One of the greatest barriers to self-assessment is the attitude that the responsibility for assessing performance and progress lies solely with the teacher. It can, therefore, sometimes be difficult to convince learners of the value of self-assessment (see the Learner's Book for further information).

We have made a distinction between assessing yourself in a practice activity and in a real-life situation. In a practice activity, the learner has more overall control; the assessment can be premeditated and the learner has time to consider carefully what to focus on. In a real-life situation, the points to be assessed are more likely to arise spontaneously rather than be preselected by the learner. We feel that learners need to be aware of these differences since practice activities can often be very unrealistic and may lead to false expectations about real-life performance.

Self-assessment can take many forms depending on such variables as the skill(s) to be assessed, the points focussed on and whether these are imposed by the teacher, the course or exam syllabus, or selected by the learners themselves. The points that learners choose to focus on will depend on their own preferences and level of satisfaction, their understanding of metalanguage, their level of awareness about both themselves and language, and their familiarity with self-assessment in general.

Learners may need clear guidance from you in establishing criteria for assessing themselves, especially in the initial stages. Becoming confident about self-assessment is a gradual process and needs to be carefully introduced in the classroom through practical demonstrations, and by regularly including opportunities for reflection, for example after specific activities or at the end of a class. This can be done by asking questions, such as, 'What did you learn from today's class?', 'Did you find this activity useful? Why or why not?' You should be prepared to be involved in a certain amount of discussion and negotiation with your learners. They will find it difficult to establish valid criteria without having observed and been involved in practical demonstrations of self-assessment in the classroom. In our experience, the more accustomed learners become to the idea of assessing themselves, the more convinced they become of its usefulness. Emphasise that whatever activities they do, whether successful or not, it is useful to keep some kind of record so that it becomes clear to them what they need to do next.

Some learners may ask questions, such as, 'Yes, but how do I know if my assessment is right?' Others may over-estimate their performance because they may be reluctant to lose face. Initially, you will need to help learners interpret their results, since it can take a while for their confidence to develop and for them to feel secure about self-assessment using their own norms rather than external ones. Try to avoid taking on the traditional role of providing learners with an assessment yourself, and make the point that self-assessment is only useful if they act upon the results. We have found that it is a good idea to introduce the concept of self-assessment with vocabulary as this seems to be more manageable for learners.

We have suggested a format for a self-assessment chart in the Learner's Book. Encourage your learners to use charts like these regularly, particularly in the initial stages. However, they may wish to adapt them or devise their own later on as they become more familiar with the concept. By keeping such records regularly, learners will be able to monitor their progress.

## 1  Points to assess

The points learners choose to focus on will depend not only on the points they chose in Step 2(2) but also on whether they are assessing their vocabulary in listening, speaking, reading or writing.

## 2  Test yourself in a practice activity

Ask your learners to read about Stig's strategy and elicit other good ways they may have of testing themselves on vocabulary.

## 3  Assess your performance in a real-life situation

Ask your learners to read what Mimi says and discuss their own experiences.

## 4  Examples

In order to give your learners an example of how to use the self-assessment chart, ask them to look at those filled in by Stig and Mimi. Encourage your learners to keep records of their progress.

■ ■ ■ ■ □ □ □

# Step 4   What do you need to do next?

| | |
|---|---|
| Materials: | Learner's Book pages 32–33 |
| Items to cover: | *Introduction*<br>Steps for setting short-term aims.<br>*Examples* |
| Time: | 15–20 minutes when you introduce setting short-term aims in this skill for the first time. Thereafter, 5–10 minute sessions when necessary. |

## Introduction

In Step 4 of the Learner's Book is a possible chart for learners to use when setting themselves short-term aims for the skills they have selected. This makes use of the results of their self-assessment in Step 3.

Ask your learners to read the Introduction in the Learner's Book. Make sure that they understand how setting short-term aims follows on from self-assessment and encourage them to use the chart suggested. Be prepared to give advice and guidance, particularly on how learners can achieve their aims (see *How* column). They will need time and experience in order to become familiar with the many strategies available to them for achieving their aims. Steps 5 and 6 will offer more suggestions.

## Examples

Encourage your learners to look carefully at the examples of how Stig and Mimi set themselves aims.

■ ■ ■ ■ □ □

# Step 5    How do you prefer to learn vocabulary?

| | |
|---|---|
| Materials: | Learner's Book pages 34–38<br>Prepared list of words<br>Carrier bag<br>Small pieces of card<br>Video camera and filming equipment (optional) |
| Items to cover: | 1. *Personal strategies*<br>   Activity: Learning new words<br>2. *Time to experiment – Grouping words*<br>   Activity: Common features<br>   Activity: Word network<br>3. *Time to experiment – Making associations*<br>   Activity: Word bag<br>   Activity: Word tour<br>   Activity: Word clip<br>4. *Choose a new strategy* |
| Time: | 40 minutes |

## 1   Personal strategies

Ask your learners to look at the comments in their books to see how some people learn new words; each one uses a different strategy. Elicit from the learners what they do and encourage an exchange of information.

### Activity: Learning new words

This experiment helps learners become more conscious of their own learning strategies and those of other members of the class.

a) Provide the learners with nine words that they are unlikely to know already. Give them five minutes to learn these words.

   You could ask your learners to work in groups of four or five and appoint an 'observer' in each group. He or she should either fill in the worksheet on page 70 or simply note down how the members of the group are learning the new words. The 'observer' will then be in a position to lead the group discussion in (d).

   Alternatively, if possible, video your class while they are learning the words. The video extract could then be shown in the follow-up session in order to sensitise learners to the variety of strategies being used. With younger learners who often get distracted very quickly, as they have short concentration spans, we have found that it is useful to give them a viewing task to focus their attention (see Fig. 3). The strategies you include on the worksheet will depend on those your learners actually use. However, if they have only a limited selection of strategies or all use similar ones, you could include others in order to make them aware that these exist.

   Here is a list of words that has been used with adult learners at intermediate level:

   | | | |
   |---|---|---|
   | huffy | belligerent | cantankerous |
   | haze | gust | flurry |
   | cantilever | gearstick | camshaft |

These words can be divided into three groups (but do not make this obvious to your learners at this point):
i)   connected with the weather
ii)  connected with machines
iii) connected with moods.

Monolingual classes can be given translations, since this is a very common way for adult learners to note down new vocabulary, but other ways of providing meaning could also be used. With secondary school learners a slightly different approach may be found useful, where you offer a variety of explanations: visual, definition, word in context, translation, etc. in order to emphasise the different ways of conveying meaning (see Fig. 4). This point can be reinforced after the experiment

## 2.1  Extending vocabulary

1. How are your classmates learning new words? Write their names in the column marked <u>Names</u>.

| <u>You</u> | <u>Are they ...</u> | <u>Names</u> |
|---|---|---|
| | working individually? | |
| | working in a small group, e.g. testing each other? | |
| | testing themselves by covering up the words or meanings? | |
| | working silently? | |
| | checking pronunciation and/or meaning with each other or with the teacher? | |
| | saying the words aloud? | |
| | saying the words silently to themselves? | |
| | copying or writing the words down? | |
| | other | |

2. Which of the ways listed in the table do you think would be the most helpful for you? Use the column on the left to put them in order of importance.
   (1 = least important, 10 = most important).

*Figure 3*

by asking the learners which kind of explanation helped them to remember best.

b) and (c) After five minutes, distract the learners' attention for a short time by discussing something different in order to disturb their short-term memory. Then ask your learners to write down as many of the words as they can remember and to consider the strategy they used for learning them.

d) Find out who was able to remember the most words. During the five minutes' learning time, you will have observed your class employing many different techniques, such as scribbling, mumbling, staring, self-testing, repeating. Use these observations to provide a starting point for the learners' discussions in groups. Encourage an exchange of experiences and ideas and ask them to consider each other's strategies.

Generally speaking, the most effective learners seem to be those who discover some kind of pattern, for example semantic groups, or those who make their own associations, for instance with a visual image in their mind. The words least likely to be remembered are those where the learner finds it difficult to provide a visual image as they may not know the word in their own language, for example 'camshaft', 'cantilever'.

Emphasise to the learners that in this activity the main focus is on their *learning strategies*, rather than on the words themselves.

## 2 Time to experiment – Grouping words

Research has shown that words are stored in the brain in connected groups, according to, for example:
- semantic associations
- stress patterns
- number of syllables
- initial consonants
- final clusters
- the type of word, e.g. noun, verb.

*Activity: Common features*

**Answers**

a) Group 1 – same initial consonant
   Group 2 – compound word
   Group 3 – same final cluster and semantic association
   Group 4 – semantic association

HOW DO YOU LEARN NEW WORDS?

You have five minutes to learn these new words.

1.  windy

2.  unpleasant                          désagréable

3.  wine                                an alcoholic drink made
                                        from grapes

4.  rabbit

5.  friendly                            kind, helpful, showing that
                                        you like someone

6.  thunderstorm                        orage

7.  heat                                'I can't walk about in this
                                        heat of 90°!'

8.  angry                               en colère

9.  necklace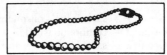

*Figure 4*

**Possible answers**

b)  i)   blackberry, strawberry, raspberry, gooseberry  −  same final
          cluster
    ii)  thyme, pear, gooseberry  −  all green
    iii) melon, lemon, walnut, currant, turkey, kitchen  −  same number
         of syllables

Find out how many different ways the class used to group the
words.

c)  Lead a class discussion.

*Activity: Word network*

This activity shows how words can be grouped by topic.

## 3   Time to experiment  −  Making associations

*Activity: Word bag*

This strategy encourages learners to process words they wish to learn by
creating their own personal associations, etc. It provides a technique for
testing oneself as well as for storing new words. (Further suggestions for
storing words can be found in Step 7.)

*Activity: Word tour*

This strategy makes use of pictorial associations. The learners imagine
vivid, often incongruous, scenes in order to remember lists of words in a
given order. This works particularly well with concrete nouns.

*Activity: Word clip*

This technique works particularly well for abstract words or colloquial
phrases.

## 4   Choose a new strategy

Encourage your learners to experiment with new strategies for learning
vocabulary in order to help them find the one(s) they prefer.

————   ■ ■ ■ ■ ■ □   ————

# Step 6   Do you need to build up your confidence?

| | |
|---|---|
| Materials: | Learner's Book pages 39–40 |
| | Cassette |
| | Collection of pictures of objects |
| | Cassette recorder and blank cassette or filming equipment (optional) |
| Items to cover: | *What can you do when you don't know a word?* |
| | Oral communication strategies, experimenting with language. |
| | Activity: Shopping |
| Time: | 40 minutes |

This Step concentrates on the active use of vocabulary in speaking. This is often the area where learners need most help in order to build up their confidence for dealing spontaneously with situations. They also use vocabulary actively when writing, but in that case it is more likely that they will have time to reflect and be able to make use of resources such as dictionaries.

Part of the Step also aims to persuade learners that playing with language, inventing new words, etc. is both valid and fun. You may need to emphasise these points, as learners often have very fixed notions about 'correct' language.

### What can you do when you don't know a word?

Play the cassette to the learners. The object being described is a Rawlplug, but do not tell your learners this — they should try to guess. (It is unlikely that they will know the word 'Rawlplug' in English, but they will probably be able to guess the word in their own language.)

Ask your learners to look at the oral communication strategies included in the chart in their books and check their comprehension. Not all of the strategies in the chart are included on the cassette and the chart itself is not exhaustive. (For further details see Riley 1985.) We have chosen to list the strategies that seem to be most accessible to learners. Play the cassette again asking learners to tick the strategies they hear the speakers using.

**Tapescript**

*Conversation 1*

*Shopkeeper*: Good morning, sir. What can I do for you?
*Customer*: Um . . . hello. Er . . . well, I don't know whether you can help me, I'm looking for a . . . I don't know what it's called. It's a small, plastic thing.
*Shopkeeper*: Er . . . plastic, sir.
*Customer*: Yeah, I think it's plastic. It's . . . it's certainly like plastic.
*Shopkeeper*: Yes.
*Customer*: Um . . . it's about half an inch by three quarters of an inch, an inch long, shaped a bit like a screw or a nail.
*Shopkeeper*: Well . . . I . . . is . . . is it a screw? . . . Is it . . .
*Customer*: No, it's not a screw.
*Shopkeeper*: Oh.
*Customer*: It's like one, the same shape um and it's sometimes pink, sometimes blue, sometimes yellow, different colours. I think the different colour means a different length.
*Shopkeeper*: Oh, I think I know what you're talking about, sir. Hold on a . . . ah . . . um . . . er . . . . Is it . . . is it . . . Is it one of these, sir?
*Customer*: Ah, that's it. That's the thing, yes. Thank you very much.

*Conversation 2*

*Shopkeeper*: Oh good morning, madam.
*Customer*: Hello . . . um . . . I've come to buy some of those um . . . those thingummies . . . Um oh, what are they called? You know, those duvries for putting in walls.
*Shopkeeper*: Duvries?
*Customer*: Yeah, the [Screws?] thingummies.
*Customer*: No, no. The thingummies that the screws go into. Sort of screwholders.
*Shopkeeper*: Screwholders? Er . . . What do they do?
*Customer*: Well you put them in the wall and you put the screws in them, and they hold the screws. You know, those . . .
*Shopkeeper*: Hold the screws in the wall? Oh! You mean er . . . You mean this sort of thing, madam?
*Customer*: That's right, yes.
*Shopkeeper*: Oh, that's it, yeah.

*Conversation 3*

*Shopkeeper*: Good morning, madam. Can I help you?
*Customer*: Yes, um, I'm looking for um, well . . . I'm . . . I'm sort of drilling a hole in the wall and I need one of those plastic things that sort of you put in the wall and then you put the na . . . the screw and sort of help it hold together in the wall. I don't know if . . . is that clear enough?
*Shopkeeper*: Mm, yes, I think I know what you mean.

**Answers**

Speaker 1: iii, iv
Speaker 2: ii, v, vi
Speaker 3: ii, iii

Ask your learners to decide which strategy or combination of strategies they thought were the most effective and why. Generally speaking, just describing an object is not enough; a combination of strategies (ii) and (iii) is likely to be the most effective. You could elicit or suggest the following points:

i)   *using a foreign word*, e.g. the target word from their own language sometimes pronounced with an English accent. This may sometimes work, but we feel it is more beneficial to encourage students to develop more adventurous strategies.

ii)  *describing what it is for*, e.g. 'it's used for pulling the cork out of a bottle' (a corkscrew). This is one of the more useful strategies.

iii) *describing what it looks like and what it is made of*, e.g. 'it's small and made of wood with four legs' (a stool). This information on its own is often not sufficient and learners can waste a lot of time and effort trying to describe objects in this way.

iv)  *using a word that is close in meaning*, e.g. 'it's a kind of chair' (a stool). This can be confusing unless it is expanded into something like 'it's a kind of chair with no back'.

v)   *inventing a new word or expression*, e.g. 'dogess' (bitch), 'dogette' (puppy), 'corkpuller' (corkscrew). This strategy is often neglected in the classroom and learners who are proficient in inventing suitable new words or expressions are often demonstrating an extensive knowledge of the language.

vi)  *using substitute words*, e.g. 'thing', 'thingy', 'thingumajig', 'thingumabob', 'thingummy'; 'whatsit', 'whatsaname'; 'doo-dah', 'duvrie'. Learners enjoy using these words, but it should be emphasised that they should not be overused, that they are informal and that they are usually only used in spoken language.

Ask the learners to think of any other strategies they could use that may be effective and add them to the list. These might include:

— mime or gesture
— sound effects
— pointing to the word in a dictionary or phrase book
— drawing the object
— showing the object.

### Activity: Shopping

Here the emphasis is on getting the learners to practise various oral communication strategies and to evaluate them.

a)   Bring into the class some pictures of objects that the learners are unlikely to know the English word for, such as funnel, kettle, dustpan, hole punch, ear plugs. (Don't tell them the English words.) You could also bring in some objects if this is feasible.

Ask your learners to work in pairs and give each pair a number of different pictures. (Tell them not to show these to anyone else.)

The type and number of objects you choose will depend on such factors as your learners' age, interests, language level, the time available. Tell them they want to buy these objects.

b) Give your learners a maximum of five minutes to prepare their strategies. Ask them *not* to use dictionaries or any other aids.

c) When they have finished collect in the object(s).

d) Learners will soon realise how effective their strategies are if their new partner is able to guess the objects in their own language.

e) The new partner should assess the strategy used.

You can give learners further practice by:
- getting them to think of objects themselves
- providing them with information-gap activities, such as describe and arrange, describe and draw, etc.
- giving them the opportunity to record or video themselves and to analyse the recording afterwards.

■ ■ ■ ■ ■ ■ ■

# Step 7 How do you organise your vocabulary learning?

| Materials: | Learner's Book pages 40–43 |
| --- | --- |
| Items to cover: | Suggestions. Vocabulary books. |
| Time: | 15 minutes |

Ask your learners to read the suggestions for organising vocabulary learning in the Learner's Book and encourage an exchange of ideas.

Ask them to consider the various ways of organising vocabulary books and to discuss these.

Encourage them to experiment with and evaluate the various systems suggested, as well as any other suggestions of their own.

**Further reading**

Aitchison, J. 1987. This book discusses the nature of the human word-store, or 'mental lexicon', and sets out to answer the questions: how do humans manage to store so many words, and how do they find the ones they want?

Bolitho, R. and Tomlinson, B. 1980. Exercises on problem areas in English for individual study or for group discussion. Unit 3 deals with vocabulary.

Carter, R. 1987. An article of major importance dealing with issues in the acquisition of vocabulary, more advanced teaching of vocabulary in context, new developments in lexicography and its implications for vocabulary teaching and study.

Channell, J. 1981. This paper describes an approach to the teaching of English vocabulary which draws on several aspects of theoretical semantics.

Dickinson, L. 1987. (See page 34.) See chapter 8.

Faerch, C. and Kasper, G. 1983. A collection of papers which examine learner interlanguage both as a linguistic system in its own right and as a means to an understanding of the language acquisition process in the context of learner-learner and learner-native speaker interaction.

Fröhlich, M. and Paribakht, T. 1984. (See page 34.) Pages 71–9 of this article discuss strategies for oral communication.

Gairns, R. and Redman, S. 1986. A practical guide for teachers on how to select, organise and teach vocabulary.

James, P. 1985. This article describes ways of recording and storing new words, in particular the 'word network' technique.

Lewkowicz, J.A. and Moon, J. 1985. This paper examines the way 'evaluation' has been defined and used in the past few decades and then considers practical ways in which evaluation can more fully involve the learner and, as a result, affect the learning process.

Lindstromberg, S. 1985. This paper discusses the use of pictorial types of schema for the teaching of vocabulary.

Oskarsson, M. 1980. An exploration of possible forms of assessment for use in adult language learning, compiled as part of the Council of Europe Modern Languages Project.

Riley, P. 1985. This paper examines the term 'strategy' by considering its definitions, etymology and use. Appendix B contains a list of communicative strategies and appendix C a list of suggested activities for developing communicative strategies. Appendix D contains a useful bibliography on communicative strategies.

Rudzka, B. et al. 1981. The aim of this book is to increase systematically the vocabulary of the intermediate and advanced learner of English. Each unit follows a system of Texts, Glosses, Discussion, Word Study and Exercises.

Rudzka, B. et al. 1985. The companion book to the above.

Smith, F. 1978. A book about the process of reading, the perceptual and language skills it involves and the nature of the task facing anyone learning to read.

Wallace, M.J. 1982. A practical guide to the teaching of vocabulary in EFL and other language teaching situations. It contains examples of different kinds of vocabulary exercises and has an answer key.

*Recommended for learners*

Davies, E. and Whitney, N. 1984. At the end of each section is a self-assessment page which encourages students to think about their work and to check their progress with specific reference to the skill of reading.

Rudzka, B. et al. 1981. (See *Further reading*.)

Rudzka, B. et al. 1985. (See *Further reading*.)
Underhill, A. 1980. (See page 53.)
Watcyn-Jones, P. 1985. There are five books in this series, from beginner to advanced
  level, containing exercises which test and teach students vocabulary in various
  topic areas. The books are suitable for classroom use, or for students working on
  their own, as each contains a key.

## 2.2 Dealing with grammar

■ ☐ ☐ ☐ ☐ ☐

## Step 1 How do you feel about learning grammar?

| | |
|---|---|
| Materials: | Learner's Book pages 44–45 |
| Items to cover: | Learners' attitudes towards grammar can affect the way they learn. |
| Time: | 15 minutes |

1. Ask your learners to consider the attitudes presented in the Learner's Book. Lead a class discussion and elicit or suggest the following points:

   *Wolfgang* reflects an awareness of some of the other aspects involved in communication. He is not obsessed by grammar, as some learners seem to be.

   *Boniface* regards grammar as the key to proficiency in the language. He sees it as a separate item and the first step in learning a language. This may reflect a past learning experience based on a structural syllabus.

   *Marjeta* is typical of a group of learners who very rarely think about their own language, which they assume to be logical and regular as they find it easy to use. Because English grammar apparently does not follow the same 'rules', they develop a negative attitude towards learning it. Such learners need to realise that English, like most other languages, operates on a system of generalisations, but that these may be different from those of other languages they know.

   *Filippo* probably represents the 'relaxed' type of learner (see 1.2). Such learners often find grammar uninteresting and difficult to relate to real-life situations. Furthermore, perhaps because of poor results in grammar tests, they may associate it with a sense of failure. This can lead to demotivation and frustration. You could tell these learners that later on they will discover that grammar can be fun.

2. and 3. Ask your learners to think about their own attitudes towards English grammar and discuss these in class. Encourage them to consider what effect these attitudes may have on their grammar learning.

■ ■ □ □ □ □

# Step 2   What do you know about English grammar?

| Materials: | Learner's Book pages 46–48 |
| --- | --- |
| | Cassette |

| Items to cover: | 1. *Languages are different* |
| --- | --- |
| | 2. *What is grammar?* |
| | Grammar as facts, patterns, choices. |
| | Activity: Using a pattern |

| Time: | 30 minutes |
| --- | --- |

## 1   Languages are different

This provides a lead in to 2: *What is grammar?* by encouraging learners to start thinking more critically about grammar. It also serves to inform you about the levels of awareness within the class about grammar and your learners' knowledge of the metalanguage necessary to discuss it.

a) Experience has shown that some learners may need more time and effort to learn English grammar than others, depending on how much grammar can be carried over from their mother tongue. Do not let these learners become demotivated by comparing their progress with that of others in the class whose own language is closer to English.

Ask your learners to consider how similar or how different the grammar of their language is compared with the grammar of English. Ask them to think of some examples and compare these with other learners. Direct them to the examples in their books. You may like to use the cassette to stimulate discussion, as this provides further examples of learners talking about the grammar of their languages.

**Tapescript**

*Beliyou (Ethiopia):* Oh, um . . . it is very different. Um . . . the word order is different. Like, um, in English, the verb'll be in the middle: subject − verb − object, but in Amharic, the verb is at the end and er the the subject, like first person, second person, third person, etc. are joined to the verb. Er . . . like, er . . . for example, in English you say, 'I can speak Amharic.' In Amharic, if you translate it, it would be, 'Amharic to speak I can.' That would be the word order − so it's different.

*David (Benin)*:  Well, I think Fon grammar is a lot different from English grammar because um in Fon all the language, I mean, most of the language is based on human bodies. For instance, um when you want to say someone goes through a door, you you say he goes through the mouth of a door.

When you want to say, for instance, I'm going to town, er . . . in Fon you say, 'I'm going inside the belly' because the belly is taken as the centre of the body . . . of human body so people think of a town as the centre of um where you are going er of the place you are going . . . so every part of language is related to er human body.

*Fumiko (Japan)*:  I think it's really quite different. I mean, Japanese is quite different from English. For example, the word order is quite opposite, um . . . such as the sentence, 'I like English.' In Japanese,

[ 私は英語が好きです。] That means, 'I English like.'

b)  Ask learners to place their language(s) on the continuum in the Learner's Book. (If you are working with Dutch or Japanese students, you could substitute German or Chinese for the languages on the continuum.)

In multilingual classes, this can provide an interesting consciousness-raising activity about the languages represented in the class. Monolingual classes can also find it valuable to discuss each other's ideas: they can then reach a class decision about where their language fits on the continuum. Draw their attention to the fact that not all learners have the same starting point for learning English grammar (see above).

## 2   What is grammar?

Many learners have a very limited concept of what grammar is. For them it is a set of complicated facts governed by rules which are full of exceptions. It is like the universe: it has no beginning, it has no end, it has no shape, it just exists and there is a lot of it! Many grammar books and, indeed, teachers do nothing to demystify grammar.

The aim of this section is to break grammar down into manageable sections which are accessible to the learner. We have chosen to use the following breakdown (Lewis, 1986: 9–12):

*Facts*
*Patterns*
*Choices*

We recommend that if you use these categories, you are consistent about referring to them whenever you deal with grammar in the classroom.

*Facts* These are non-generative and cannot be applied generally, for example the plural of 'woman' is 'women' not 'womans'. Once learners are aware of this category, they can be encouraged simply to accept the facts for what they are and learn them, rather than waste time worrying about them or challenging them. Encourage learners to take on responsibility for learning these in their own time.

*Patterns* This area can be dealt with fruitfully in the classroom, since learners may need to be trained and encouraged to look for patterns. Once a pattern has been noted, encourage learners to generate new language from it (see the activity below.) This type of activity is confidence-boosting and motivating, as learners can see they are covering a lot of ground. We recommend it be done in groups, where it can provide a meaningful, communicative exercise.

*Choices* Learners are not often aware that the use of certain grammatical forms is a matter of personal choice. They believe there is a rule which governs each situation. A familiar question is 'Which one is right?' when both or all are grammatically correct. Learners need quite a long time and a lot of exposure to language before they develop a deep understanding of the relationship between grammar and meaning and its subtle distinctions. Encourage your learners to read and listen to English as much as possible for examples of grammar in context. In the classroom, encourage discussion about choices and subtle differences in meaning.

### Activity: Using a pattern

Ask your learners to generate new language from the example provided or from one of your own. Write the examples on the board or overhead projector in order to show the wide range of possibilities. Point out to the learners that in order to generate new language they need to have understood the pattern.

You should be on the look-out to check that the original pattern is used. Any deviation, such as 'I love swimming in the sea', can be used in class to promote discussion; this will generally be extremely worthwhile and often amusing.

Suggest that your class build up a Pattern Bank (see Step 5).

■ ■ ■ □ □ □ □

# Step 3   How well are you doing?

| Materials: | Learner's Book pages 48–50 |
|---|---|
| | Examples of mistakes from learners' work |

| Items to cover: | 1. *Points to assess* |
|---|---|
| | Assessing mistakes. |
| | 2. *Test yourself in a practice activity* |
| | 3. *Assess your performance in a real-life situation* |
| | 4. *Examples* |

| Time: | 35 minutes when you introduce self-assessment in this skill for the first time. Thereafter, 5–10 minute sessions when necessary. |
|---|---|

If you are doing a Step 3 for the first time, read the introduction on pages 65–7 in *2.1 Extending vocabulary*. If your learners are doing a Step 3 for the first time, refer them to page 30 in *2.1 Extending vocabulary* in the Learner's Book.

## 1   Points to assess

a)  Learners are often obsessed with being correct all the time in their use of grammar. This is unrealistic and they quickly become demotivated when they find themselves making what we might call silly slips. They may never have considered the relative seriousness of the grammatical mistakes they make and may classify them all as very serious. This activity aims to encourage them to evaluate grammatical mistakes and to decide for themselves what they want to concentrate on when selecting their points to assess. Learners rarely agree on 'seriousness' as this depends on how correct each individual wants to be and what his or her aims are, etc. Respect each learner's point of view and ask what this says about his or her approach to learning English.

You may wish to choose other examples of your own from your learners' work since speakers of different languages make different types of mistakes.

Elicit or suggest the following points in a class discussion:

i)  *Mistake*: work     *Correct form*: works
    Learners will probably come to the conclusion that this is not a very serious mistake; it is often a slip of the tongue and is unlikely to cause confusion.

ii) *Mistake*: Where you go?   *Correct form*: Where are you going?
Where did you go?
Confusion is caused because the tense is uncertain. In some circumstances, the context might provide a clue, but not necessarily, so this is a fairly serious mistake.

iii) *Mistake*: I've been cutting   *Correct form*: I've cut
The speaker has not understood the meaning associated with the progressive verb form in this particular situation. In other words, the notion of an action repeated over a period of time or a general recent activity, e.g. 'I've been chopping wood'. The example in the Learner's Book sounds bizarre and could cause concern about the mental stability of the speaker!

iv) *Mistake*: from   *Correct form*: on
Learners get very worried about making mistakes with prepositions and, indeed, they can be a problem in English. Reassure them that generally these mistakes are not as serious as they might think and are unlikely to cause a major misunderstanding.

v) *Mistake*: What means . . . ?   *Correct form*: What does
'flabbergasted'
mean?
In the classroom, this mistake may not be very serious because the meaning is clear. However, it could be important for your learners to get question forms right outside the classroom, particularly when asking for specific information, where a confused question form could cause problems, or in a situation where time is limited.

b) In most everyday situations, when speaking, you get immediate feedback and a chance to explain further, so accuracy may not be so essential. One situation where accuracy in speaking is essential would be a pilot talking to Air Traffic Control.

c) The list of suggested points to assess is by no means exhaustive. The learners may need to discuss appropriate points with you and, indeed, may wish to use different ones. In some cases, the use of metalanguage, as in our suggested list, may not be appropriate for your learners.

Remind learners to select no more than two or three points to focus on for any one self-assessment, and point out that it is generally more important to be accurate when writing. Some exceptions to this may be personal writing, such as a diary or a shopping list, or informal notes and messages, where the most important factor is that the information should be clear.

## 2   Test yourself in a practice activity

Delia's strategy for testing herself is probably the most usual and convenient. Learners need to be aware of suitable materials to choose from, and you may be able to recommend a variety of sources (see *Recommended for learners*).

## 3   Assess your performance in a real-life situation

Ask your learners to read what Khaled says and discuss their own experiences.

## 4   Examples

In order to give your learners an example of how to use the self-assessment chart, ask them to look at those filled in by Delia and Khaled. Encourage your learners to keep records of their progress.

———   ■ ■ ■ ■ □ □ □   ———

# Step 4   What do you need to do next?

| | |
|---|---|
| Materials: | Learner's Book pages 50–51 |
| Items to cover: | Examples of learners' short-term aims. |
| Time: | 15–20 minutes when you introduce setting short-term aims in this skill for the first time. Thereafter, 5–10 minute sessions when necessary. |

If you are doing a Step 4 for the first time, read pages 67–8 in *2.1 Extending vocabulary*. If your learners are doing a Step 4 for the first time, refer them to page 32 in *2.1 Extending vocabulary* in the Learner's Book. They should then look at the examples of how Delia and Khaled set themselves short-term aims.

■ ■ ■ ■ ■ □ □

# Step 5   How do you prefer to learn grammar?

| Materials: | Learner's Book pages 51–52 |
| --- | --- |
| | Cassette |
| Items to cover: | 1. *Personal strategies* |
| | 2. *Suggestions* |
| | Pattern Banks, Discuss grammar. |
| | 3. *Choose a new strategy* |
| Time: | 25 minutes |

## 1   Personal strategies

Ask your learners to read about the strategies used by Pedro, Leah and Yasmeen and check their comprehension. Elicit from the learners what they do and encourage an exchange of ideas.

*Pedro* seems to be interested in grammar as well as reading and realises that authentic materials are an important source. Notice how he cuts out the paragraphs to keep the grammar examples in context.

*Leah* is exploiting the expertise of native speakers around her. Notice how she specifies what sort of mistakes she wants them to correct her on. Point out to learners that native speakers will often not correct mistakes unless asked, as this may seem impolite.

*Yasmeen* has found an alternative method of making use of her grammar book and exercises. It does not occur to many students that exercises can be used for anything other than testing themselves, but she is learning by doing.

## 2   Suggestions

a)   Take your learners through the steps for building up a Pattern Bank.

b)   Point out the usefulness of discussing grammar points and sharing ideas. The cassette provides an example of two learners, Chen from China and Kasuko from Japan, discussing the grammar of the following two sentences:

'I lived in London for ten years.'
'I have lived in London for ten years.'

You can encourage your learners to discuss grammar in a similar way by providing them with examples of pairs of sentences to look at.

### Tapescript

*Chen*:  I'm not sure about these past tenses 'lived' and 'have lived'. Do you know?

*Kasuko*:  Um, well, I'm not sure either but um maybe um  . . .

*Chen*:  Yes, so what's the difference between these two sentences, 'I've lived in London for 10 years'  . . .

*Kasuko*:  'Live' is a past tense . . . 'Lived' is a past tense, but 'have lived' is not a past tense . . .

*Chen*:  Yeah, I know, I know, but er the meaning? Any difference? The meaning . . .

*Kasuko*:  Yes. 'Have lived' would be um a sort of duration of um until the present, from the past period until the present. Is that right?

*Chen*:  Well, er . . . probably. I should think so, but 'I lived in London for 10 years' . . . is it not until the present?

*Kasuko*:  I don't think so. Maybe um, some time ago I was living in London and it is a fact that I lived in London and how long was [no] it then . . . maybe 10 years.

*Chen*:  So you mean you lived in London before [I . . . ] but er now you . . .

*Kasuko*:  No, now I don't live in London.

*Chen*:  Oh, so you mean the difference between the two sentence is that this one you moved out of London . . .

*Kasuko*:  Yes.

*Chen*:  So you use 'lived' . . .

*Kasuko*:  Yes, so 'I have lived' would be 'I'm still in London.' Is that right?

*Chen*:  Oh I should think so . . . well shall we just call . . .

*Kasuko*:  Ask our tutor?

## 3   Choose a new strategy

Encourage the learners to experiment with new strategies for dealing with grammar in order to help them find the one(s) they prefer.

■■■■■□

# Step 6   Do you need to build up your confidence?

| Materials: | Learner's Book pages 52–54<br>Cassette |
|---|---|
| Items to cover: | *Discovering the pattern or rule*<br>Activity: Some and any<br>Activity: The human computer |
| Time: | 30 minutes |

**Discovering the pattern or rule**

This section encourages learners to try out discovery learning. We
recommend you use this approach from time to time, as it can help
learners develop a deeper understanding of grammar and is more
memorable for them. Avoid giving explanations as much as possible and
allow learners to experiment. This approach may be different from what
they are used to and from the requirements of the syllabus. Nevertheless,
some time spent on discovery learning can help learners develop their
thinking capacity, build up their confidence and take responsibility for
dealing with grammar.

*Activity: Some and any*

This is an activity to put discovery learning into practice. Learners are
asked to devise their own rule for the use of *some* and *any*.

a)  Ask learners to look at the three examples in their books and discuss
    and formulate a rule. They will probably say:

    *any* is used for questions and negatives
    *some* is used for positive statements.

b)  Now give learners these examples:
    –  I like some pop music.
    –  I like any pop music.
    –  I don't like some pop music.
    –  I don't like any pop music.
    Ask learners to reconsider their rule and check it.

These examples are taken directly from Lewis (1986:33–5).

Both *some* and *any* are used with indefinite reference.
    *Some* is used if the idea is *restricted* or *limited* in some way.
    *Any* is used if the idea is *unrestricted* or *unlimited*.
    *Any* applies to all or none; *some* applies to part.

Lewis uses the following diagrams to illustrate this point.

≫→

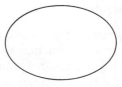

This diagram represents all the pop music in the world.

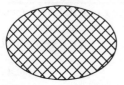

**I like any pop music**

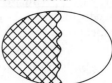

**I like some pop music**

**I don't like any pop music**

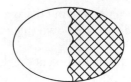

**I don't like some pop music**

The shaded areas represent the pop music liked.

### Activity: The human computer*

In many classroom situations grammar activities can be quite stressful for some learners as the focus is usually on being correct. This activity removes the stressful element because no judgement is passed by the teacher on the learners' performance.

By becoming the 'human computer', the teacher distances him or herself from the role of assessor and allows the learners the freedom to practise grammatical structures without having to worry about making mistakes. The feedback from the human computer, in the form of the correct response, encourages learners to listen carefully and to formulate their own hypotheses as to why their suggestions were right or wrong. This gives them active practice in self-assessment and experimenting and makes the grammar point more memorable.

We have found that this activity works well in large classes and that it can be used as part of a controlled practice, as remedial practice or, in some cases, as a presentation activity.

You will need to demonstrate this game to your learners, as described in the Learner's Book. Sometimes learners' suggestions, like that of Learner 3, will be a little bizarre. Try to give a correct example as close in meaning as possible.

*Dutra, 1985

The first time you try this activity the learners may be a little shy but, as they become more accustomed to the technique, you could ask them to prepare a certain grammatical point and then choose one of them to be the human computer. Another learner could also act as the 'computer programmer' and monitor the correctness of the versions given by the human computer. He or she would have to 'reprogram' the computer if it made a mistake by explaining its mistake and providing the correct response.

The cassette provides a recording of a classroom session of 'The human computer'. You could use this to demonstrate the game to your students.

**Tapescript**

*Learner*:  She is awarded a prize.
*Computer*:  She was awarded a prize.

*Learner*:  The flowers were picked.
*Computer*:  The flowers were picked.

*Learner*:  The cat ate the mouse.
*Computer*:  The mouse was eaten by the cat.

*Learner*:  He killed the man.
*Computer*:  The man was killed.

*Learner*:  He stole the car.
*Computer*:  The car was stolen.

*Learner*:  Her dress was stained by the red wine.
*Computer*:  Her dress was stained by the red wine.

■■■■■■■

# Step 7    How do you organise your grammar learning?

| Materials: | Learner's Book page 54 |
|---|---|
| Items to cover: | Suggestions. |
| Time: | 10 minutes |

Ask your learners to read the suggestions in the Learner's Book for organising grammar learning and encourage an exchange of ideas.

**Further reading**

Bolitho, R. and Tomlinson, B. 1980. (See page 78.)

Chalker, S. 1984. A reference grammar identifying and explaining the components of English grammar for teachers and advanced students.

Close, R.A. 1981. A reference grammar with clear explanations and illustrated by numerous examples and diagrams.

Lewis, M. 1986. This book assesses the central role of grammar exploration in a modern communicative approach and leads the reader through a step-by-step exploration of the structure of the English verb.

Swan, M. and Smith, B. (eds.) 1987. This is a practical reference book which compares the relevant features of the learners' own languages with English, helping teachers to predict and understand the problems their learners have.

*Recommended for learners*

Blissett, C. and Hallgarten, K. 1985. A useful first grammar book with clear layout and content.

Murphy, R. 1985. (See page 53.)

Shepherd, J. et al. 1986. A grammar reference and practice book for post-elementary to higher-intermediate students.

## 2.3  Listening

—— ■ ☐ ☐ ☐ ☐ ☐ ——————————

## Step 1  How do you feel about listening to English?

| | |
|---|---|
| Materials: | Learner's Book page 55 |
| Items to cover: | Learners' attitudes towards listening to English can affect the way they learn. |
| Time: | 15 minutes |

1. Lead a class discussion about the attitudes presented in the Learner's Book. Elicit or suggest the following points:

   *Somsamai* reflects the attitude typical of many learners who think that they need to understand every word, indeed; many have been trained to listen in this way. However this can lead to much frustration both in and outside the classroom (see Step 2 for practice in listening strategies).

   *Soraya* shows a very positive attitude which should enable her to be very open-minded about any problems she may encounter when she listens to English.

   *Paul*'s attitude is more realistic than Somsamai's because he realises 100% comprehension is not necessary and he also makes use of paralinguistic clues to meaning.

2. and 3. Ask your learners to think about their own attitudes towards listening to English and to discuss these in class. Encourage them to consider what effect these attitudes may have on their listening.

■ ■ □ □ □ □ □

# Step 2   What do you know about listening to English?

| Materials: | Learner's Book pages 56–58 |
|---|---|
| | Cassette |
| | *Video English* (British Council and Macmillan) |
| | Cassette 2 Sequence 5.2 (optional) |
| | *Task Listening* (Blundell and Stokes) Unit 22 (optional) |

| Items to cover: | 1. *Listening to native speakers of English* |
|---|---|
| | English is a stress-timed language. |
| | Activity: Guessing what a conversation is about |
| | 2. *Listening strategies* |
| | Listening for gist, selecting and rejecting. |
| | Activity: Reasons for listening |

| Time: | 45–50 minutes |
|---|---|

We recommend that this unit is integrated as far as possible into a listening activity (see the lesson plan on page 24). In our experience, learners are often unaware of much of the information which you will be providing for them and are fascinated by it, as it gives them insights into the reasons for their problems and motivates them to listen. In this way, it can provide a good starting point for a listening skills based activity.

## 1   Listening to native speakers of English

Play the cassette of Marie-Claude asking for directions in London and elicit responses to the question, 'What problems is she having?'

**Possible answers**

She can't understand because:
– the native speaker is speaking too fast
– the native speaker is swallowing his words
– too much information is given
– she is unfamiliar with the words used
– she is unfamiliar with the accent of the speaker.

Encourage discussion and ask your learners if they ever have any problems like Marie-Claude's.

**Tapescript**

*Marie Claude*:  Er, excuse me please, er . . .
*Native Speaker*:  Yeah?
*Marie Claude*:  Er, excuse me, where is, er Regent Street?
*Native Speaker*:  What?
*Marie Claude*:  Er, Regent Street?
*Native Speaker*:  Oh, Regent Street.
*Marie Claude*:  Er, yes, yes.
*Native Speaker*:  Er, well, look, you go up to the top of the street, right?
   Turn left, carry straight on, you'll see the tube station on your right . . .
*Marie Claude*:  Yes.
*Native Speaker*:  Yeah? Go past that, turn left and you'll have Regent Street.
   You can't miss it. All right?
*Marie Claude*:  Thank you very much.

*Variation*:   Use *Video English* Cassette 2, Sequence 5.2 instead of the
cassette.

At this point, take on the role of informant. The reason why English
speakers may appear to speak too fast and 'swallow' their words is
because English is *stress-timed*.

Demonstrate what 'stress-timed' means by putting the four sentences
from the Learner's Book on the board or an overhead projector and playing the cassette. This is based on Mortimer (1985:76).

Emphasise the regular beat and the stressed words by clapping or tap-
ping, etc.

Play the cassette again and ask the learners to say what happens to the
pronunciation of words between the stressed words.

Explain to the class how the pronunciation of the unstressed syllables
changes as they have to be fitted in between the stressed ones. These
changes are called *weak forms*. The vowel sounds are often reduced to a
sound called 'schwa' which looks like this in phonetic script /ə/. Point out
to learners that it is this change in pronunciation which accounts for their
not being able to *hear* every word. Ask your learners if their language(s)
is/are stress-timed.

With younger learners it is fun to divide the class into four groups and
give each group one of the four sentences to chant. Group 1 starts off
with the first sentence, 1 2 3 4, in order to establish the rhythm. The other
groups join in one by one until the whole class is chanting. Half a minute
for this activity is usually enough as it can get quite noisy!

Play the extract of Marie-Claude again and ask learners what the
native speaker says, starting from, 'Well look,' to 'right?' (see tapescript).
Put the sentence on the board or overhead projector and elicit from the
learners:

– the stressed words, marking these (see below)
– the weak forms.

'Well look, you go up to the top of the street, right?'

Ask what kind of words are stressed. Elicit the answer: words which carry the *meaning*. Demonstrate this by saying:

**up      top      street**

As the meaning is clear, the other words are not necessary.

Ask the learners to consider how this information can help them with their listening. Emphasise the following advice for listening to English:

i)   Don't panic!
ii)  Don't expect to hear every single word (100% comprehension is not necessary – native-speaker listeners operate on a partial, reasonable interpretation.)
iii) Listen for the stressed words.

### Activity: Guessing what a conversation is about

This activity may be used now or at a later stage. We recommend it is covered, however, as it both consolidates the preceding activities and presents new information.

a)   Ask your learners to look at the pictures and identify possible topics. Then play the cassette and ask them to match the conversations with the pictures.

b)   The learners should compare answers with each other. Don't give them the answers yet.

c)   Ask the learners to make a note of the words that helped them to guess the topics of the conversations while they listen to the cassette for a second time.
     Discuss the learners' answers, elicit the words they have noted and put them on the board or overhead projector. (These will generally be words that the speakers stressed.) Doing this can be motivating for the learners because they can see how many words they in fact know. Use this opportunity to clarify meanings and work on pronunciation, where appropriate.

d)   We have found that for most learners the conversation about London is the easiest to understand. Elicit the following possible reasons from your learners, or suggest them yourself.

*Previous knowledge*:  they already know a little about London and probably have a stereotyped picture in their mind. The conversation corresponds with their expectations; the more they know in advance, the less they need to hear.

*Repetition*:   many ideas and words are repeated. This is a typical feature of normal everyday conversation in English. Point out to the learners that this can help them when listening to conversations, for example, on the radio. If they miss something the first time, they will probably have another chance. (You might like to contrast this with a news broadcast, for example, where the language has been carefully scripted.)

*Familiar vocabulary*:   the vocabulary used, in fact, is fairly limited and not in any way specialised.

e)   We have found most learners find the conversation about the lawnmower the most difficult. Again, you should elicit or suggest the following possible reasons.

*No prior knowledge of the context*:   the lawnmower is not actually named and they can't see the 'it' referred to on the recording. There may therefore be some confusion with the picture of the broken-down motorcycle. Point out to learners how important the visual element can be as an aid to understanding in real-life conversations.

*Unfamiliar vocabulary*:   that is, unknown words which are vital for understanding. Point out how important preparation for listening can be. For example, before listening to a radio programme on a specific topic, learners could spend some time studying the relevant vocabulary.

**Tapescript**

*Conversation 1*

A:  She doesn't like a great deal of exercise, maybe once, twice a day, oh, particularly in the evenings after she's eaten.

B:  Right. How far shall I take her?

A:  Oh, maybe half a mile but, I mean don't worry too much, a quarter of a mile if you are lucky, then she'll drag you back!

B:  Yes, and is that when she goes to the toilet?

A:  That's when she goes to the toilet. The important thing about that is don't give water late at night, obviously if you give water late at night, you'll be up half the night yourself, because she'll be pawing at the door and trying to get out.

B:  OK, got that.

A:  Or you'll find a little puddle! Ha, ha, ha! Um, about eating, just one big meal per day.

B:  Yes.

A:  About, you know, maybe one can or a can and a half . . .

B:  So, one of these big tins here.

A:  That's right. One of those big tins, you can get them down Tesco's, somewhere like that, um . . . but I've provided half a dozen tins to be starting out with, so there you go.

B: Fine.
A: Great.

Conversation 2

A: So did you and boys have a good day out then?
B: Oh it was great, [Oh!] it was really lovely.
A: Tell us about it, eh?
B: Well, when we got off the train we went and er . . . did some shopping, we had a look at the shops and . . .
A: Oh, aren't they lovely?
B: Oh, they were lovely, I mean they have got so much stock in, you know.
A: Yes, much more than we have here.
B: Oh and it's so colourful you know, all the clothes, and the food and everything, it's lovely. And then after that we had a walk in the park which was beautiful [they are] they are nice, I mean [flowers and everything] it's like being in the country [yeah, yeah] in those parks you know with the ducks, and then we had um a spot of lunch [mm] that was nice, and then after that, we went to the Tower [Oh!] and, oh it's magnificent [Yes, it is] isn't it? Have you been? [It is, it's wonderful. Real history.] Yes, we saw the Crown Jewels, and that was exciting for the boys, they thought that was wonderful and then . . .
A: Did you go to the Palace at all?
B: Yes we went to the Palace and we stood outside the gates [Yes] and looked in, but we didn't see the Queen. [No] I don't think she was there.
A: But you really had a good day?
B: Oh we had a great time.
A: Oh, would you go again?
B: Oh, certainly. Yes, next holiday.
A: Lovely!

Conversation 3

A: What's the matter with it then?
B: I don't know. I've been working out here for hours and then suddenly it stopped, I don't know why it stopped.
A: Well, have you checked the engine?
B: Well, I had a look at the spark plug, then I had a look at the lead, then I thought I'd better take the plug out and clean it, but that still didn't make it work.
A: Mm, what are you going to do now?
B: Well, I don't know. I suppose I'd better take the side cover off . . .
A: Mm.
B: See if anything's jamming it up there.
A: Yep.
B: Then I may have to look at the carburettor to see if the petrol's coming through.
A: Yes, that sounds like a good idea.
B: Er well, mm.

**Answers**

1.   The man with the dog
2.   Tower of London
3.   Lawnmower

*Variation*:   Use *Task Listening* Unit 22.

## 2   Listening strategies

Ask your learners to think about possible situations where they might use the strategies mentioned. Elicit suggestions, for example:

*Listening for gist*: turning on the radio and listening to find out what the programme is about.
*Selecting and rejecting*: listening to a station announcement to find out which platform your train leaves from.

Point out that it is unusual to need to understand every word of what you are listening to, unless you are listening, for example, to some specific instructions, or to an important message that you must pass on to someone else.

### *Activity: Reasons for listening*

This gives learners an opportunity to practise the strategies mentioned. Play the cassette and then ask the learners to discuss the listening strategies they used and why.

a) Learners will probably first listen for gist to find out what the recipe is. If they decide they will use it, they will no doubt need to listen again in detail, in order to write it down.

#### Tapescript

Now let's have a look at the recipe today and it's called 'Sausage Surprise'. It's a way of turning just ordinary sausage and potatoes into something really rather interesting, and before you say, 'Ah ah, the surprise is there are no sausages in it', I'll tell you that the first ingredient is a pound of pork sausages, a pound of pork sausages, and you need to slice the sausages into probably, each sausage into three. So you put all the sausages in the bottom of a casserole dish. And then you take an onion, er, a good-sized onion, and peel it and slice it, and lay the slices of onion over the top of the sausages. Now you'll need the can opener, easy recipe this one, it's got a tin of tomatoes in it, a 14½ ounce tin of tomatoes. Open the tin and pour the tomatoes and the juice over the top of the sausage and onions.

Good so far?

So take now some salt and pepper to flavour it. I like lashings of black pepper on mine, and, if you like, some mixed herbs as well, they give an added little flavour to it. Very nice. So some mixed herbs and salt and pepper to taste. And now we come to the potatoes, I think you need about four big potatoes for this recipe and slice them, I should peel them or scrub them first I suppose, and slice them and lay them over the top of the other ingredients. So that's four good-sized potatoes. And then you need about six ounces of cheese to be grated, six ounces of cheese, I use Cheddar cheese usually, and you grate that, put that over the top and then pop it in the oven. The oven will need to be at gas mark four and you cook it very slowly, for about two and a half hours, and when you bring it out the cheese on top'll be golden brown, everything will be bubbling away and there's a lovely smell when this recipe's cooking, really is a lovely smell and you'll have your Sausage Surprise!

b) This practises the technique of selecting and rejecting.

**Tapescript**

Hello Empire Cinema. This is a recorded message with details of programmes for today.

Screen 1 is showing *A Handful of Dust*. PG certificate. Doors open at 1.45, 4.45, 7.45. Programmes commence at 2.05, 5.05 and 8.05 and *A Handful of Dust* at 2.35, 5.35 and 8.35. Sunday programmes are at 5.05 and 8.05. Price of admission for adults is £2.40 pence, children £1.30 and family concessions throughout applicable.

—— ■ ■ ■ ☐ ☐ ☐ ☐ ——————————

# Step 3   How well are you doing?

| | |
|---|---|
| Materials: | Learner's Book pages 59–60<br>Information about local resources (recordings, radio programmes etc.) |
| Items to cover: | 1. *Points to assess*<br>2. *Test yourself in a practice activity*<br>3. *Assess your performance in a real-life situation*<br>4. *Examples* |
| Time: | 15–20 minutes when you introduce self-assessment in this skill for the first time. Thereafter, 5–10 minute sessions when necessary. |

If you are doing a Step 3 for the first time, read pages 65–7 in *2.1 Extending vocabulary*. If your learners are doing a Step 3 for the first time, refer them to page 30 in *2.1 Extending vocabulary* in the Learner's Book.

## 1   Points to assess

To help learners select their points to assess, tell them that they should be clear both about their reason for listening and about what they are listening to (see Step 2(2)). They may assess their listening comprehension according to the points listed in the Learner's Book, and by asking themselves the questions suggested.

## 2   Test yourself in a practice activity

Ask your learners to read Micheline's comments and check their comprehension. When listening, learners may find it easy to decide whether they have understood or not; this is a spontaneous and subconscious process. The aim is to go beyond the 'Yes, I did understand' or 'No, I didn't understand' stage, and encourage learners to analyse what and why they didn't understand and what they can do to help themselves. Sometimes it is difficult for learners to find suitable materials for practising this self-assessment. You could refer them to local resources at this point.

Elicit ideas from learners. These may be rather limited, so here are some further suggestions you could make:
— Foreign students at English-speaking universities who need to listen to lectures could listen to recordings of lectures in the language laboratory or self-access centre, or at home if cassettes are available for loan. They should start with short extracts and build up to longer ones. They could take notes while listening and try to do this without stopping the tape. They should then listen again and check these notes for the main points.
— Learners could arrange with a friend to listen to the news in English on the radio or TV on a particular day. They could report back to each other and compare whether they have all of the main points.
— If learners are planning to visit a certain English-speaking region, e.g. N. Ireland, Texas, Glasgow, they could check if they can understand the local accent by listening to recordings of speakers from that area. If they cannot understand much, they should listen again and keep testing themselves. (A useful source is Hughes and Trudgill, 1979.)

## 3   Assess your performance in a real-life situation

Ask learners to read Santiago's comments and discuss their own experiences.

## 4   Examples

In order to give your learners an example of how to use the self-assessment chart, ask them to look at those filled in by Micheline and Santiago. Encourage your learners to keep records of their progress.

■ ■ ■ ■ □ □ □

# Step 4   What do you need to do next?

| | |
|---|---|
| Materials: | Learner's Book page 61 |
| Items to cover: | Examples of learners' short-term aims. |
| Time: | 15–20 minutes when you introduce setting short-term aims in this skill for the first time. Thereafter, 5–10 minute sessions when necessary. |

If you are doing a Step 4 for the first time, read pages 67–8 in *2.1 Extending vocabulary*. If your learners are doing a Step 4 for the first time, refer them to page 32 in *2.1 Extending vocabulary* in the Learner's Book. They should then look at the examples of how Micheline and Santiago set themselves short-term aims.

■ ■ ■ ■ ■ □ □

# Step 5   How do you prefer to practise your listening?

| | |
|---|---|
| Materials: | Learner's Book pages 62–63<br>Cassette |
| Items to cover: | 1. *Personal strategies*<br>2. *Time to experiment*<br>    Activity: How to take control<br>3. *Choose a new strategy* |
| Time: | 25 minutes |

## 1   Personal strategies

Ask your learners to read the comments and check their comprehension. Elicit from the learners what they do and encourage an exchange of ideas.

## 2   Time to experiment

*Activity: How to take control*

a) This activity encourages learners to become aware of and practise such communication strategies as:

| | |
|---|---|
| making appeals | Can you speak a little slower, please? |
| asking for repetition/clarification | Can you say that again, please? I'm sorry? What is . . . (flint)? |
| repeating information | number 202, 19 the second road on the right |
| checking/confirming | two hundred? by the? I take the . . . Did you say . . . ? |
| reformulating | ah, the . . . ('bar' for 'public house') the second . . . ('road' for 'turning') |
| summarising | So, can I repeat to you please? |

Play the cassette of Pieter from Holland talking to his English friend Jane and go through the questions in the Learner's Book.

### Tapescript

*Pieter*: So can you explain to me please how I am coming to your house?
*Jane*: Yes, yes of course. Get the number two o two (202) bus which is outside the station.
*Pieter*: Oh, oh please. I'm sorry, can you er . . . speak a little slower, please?
*Jane*: Oh sorry, [Thank you.] yes. Um, you go to your railway station.
*Pieter*: Yah.
*Jane*: And you get the number two hundred and two bus.
*Pieter*: S . . . I'm s . . . Two hundred?
*Jane*: Two hundred and two.
*Pieter*: Two hundred and two.
*Jane*: It stops outside the station.
*Pieter*: Mm, mm.
*Jane*: And come into our village. Get off the bus in the middle of the village by the pub . . .
*Pieter*: By the?
*Jane*: Public house, it's called, er, er . . . by the public house – that sells beer.
*Pieter*: Ah, by . . . er the bar.
*Jane*: The bar, that's right, yes, and then carry on in the direction the bus is going.

*Pieter*:  I'm sorry?

*Jane*:  Um, continue up the road the way the bus goes.

*Pieter*:  Did you say I continue with the bus or . . .

*Jane*:  Yes with the bus.

*Pieter*:  But not on the bus.

*Jane*:  No, no, no, no. Get off the bus and er continue in the same direction the bus is going . . .

*Pieter*:  Ah yah, I see.

*Jane*:  And you take the te . . . the second turning on the right by a very tall . . .

*Pieter*:  I'm sorry, I take the second?

*Jane*:  Second turning on the right . . .

*Pieter*:  The second road on the right.

*Jane*:  Yes, second road on the right .

*Pieter*:  Yah, OK.

*Jane*:  By a very tall flint wall and . . .

*Pieter*:  A . . . a flint wall.

*Jane*:  A flint yes. It's a . . .

*Pieter*:  What is a flint?

*Jane*:  It's a stone, stone wall, a very, very tall stone wall . . .

*Pieter*:  Ah yah, OK.

*Jane*:  And then carry on down the lane, um . . . round the right-angled bend . . .

*Pieter*:  I'm sorry, can you say that again please?

*Jane*:  Yes, you carry on, you go down the lane, walk down the lane and then there's a, a curve, a right-angle curve . . .

*Pieter*:  Yah.

*Jane*:  You carry on for 300 yards . . .

*Pieter*:  Yah.

*Jane*:  And then our house is on the left, it's number 19 . . .

*Pieter*:  Number 90.

*Jane*:  19.

*Pieter*:  Ah, 19.

*Jane*:  Yes.

*Pieter*:  OK.

*Jane*:  Opposite some very tall gates.

*Pieter*:  OK, so can I repeat to you please?

*Jane*:  Yes.

*Pieter*:  Um, I . . . I am on the number two hundred and two bus.

*Jane*:  Yes.

*Pieter*:  I get off. Where am I getting off?

*Jane*:  At the public house.

*Pieter*:  At the public house, the bar, yah, and I'm walking in the direction of the bus and then on the second turning on the right I am walking down the road round a curve.

*Jane*:  That's right.

*Pieter*:  Yah and then I am by a big gates, there's a house on the left, number 19.

*Jane*:  That's right.

*Pieter*:  Good, I see you in maybe two hours or so yah?

*Jane*:  Yes lovely, bye bye. [Thank you.]

*Pieter*:  Bye.

b) Dictate a short message to your class and encourage them to interrupt you, using the strategies they have heard, in order to ensure that they write the message down correctly.

## 3  Choose a new strategy

Encourage the learners to experiment with new strategies for practising their listening in order to help them find the one(s) they prefer.

■ ■ ■ ■ ■ □

# Step 6   Do you need to build up your confidence?

| Materials: | Learner's Book pages 63–64 |
| --- | --- |
| | Cassette |
| | Recording of news in learners' language(s) |
| | Recording of news in English |
| | Newspapers in learners' language(s) or English |
| Items to cover: | 1. *Preparing and predicting* |
| | Activity: Listening to the news |
| | 2. *How we predict* |
| | Activity: Can you predict in English? |
| Time: | 45 minutes |

## 1  Preparing and predicting

Ask your learners to read the information in the Learner's Book.

### Activity: Listening to the news

This can be done in class or as a self-study activity. It aims to help learners build up their confidence for listening by encouraging them to prepare themselves in advance. It also gives them practice in the strategy of selecting and rejecting (see Step 2(2)) according to their own interests.

If you decide to do this activity in class, you may wish to bring in a recording of the news in English, a recording of the news in the learners' language, and newspapers in English and/or the learners' language(s).

## 2   How we predict

Ask your learners to read the information in the Learner's Book. If you think it is useful, they could practise predicting in their own language by finishing each other's sentences, for example. Point out that their ability to predict in English will depend on the factors listed in the Learner's Book. Go through these, checking comprehension.

### Activity: Can you predict in English?

The aim of this exercise is to help learners become aware of the many clues that they can use as an aid to understanding in addition to the visual element.

a)   The examples are presented to ensure that the learners understand what is required of them in this activity.

**Tapescript and answers**

i)     For breakfast, I always have eggs and [bacon]. (Or any other breakfast food, e.g. sausages, toast.)

ii)    My brother's got two dogs and three [cats]. (Or any other pet.)

b)   Play the cassette and allow time for the learners to compare their predictions.

c)   Play the complete sentences, so that the learners can check their answers. Elicit from them the factors which helped them predict and play the cassette again if necessary.

**Tapescript and answers**

i)    *Situation*: tired-sounding person, possibly husband talking to wife after he has come home from a hard day at the office
'Oh, what a day! I'm exhausted! What I really need now is a good, strong cup of . . . [coffee].' (Or any other beverage that is drunk from a cup and is reviving.)

ii)   *Situation*: in a baker's (sales assistant to customer)
*Background noises*: shop, customers
'A large white loaf? Oh, I'm terribly sorry, I'm afraid . . . [we're sold out].' (Or any other appropriate response meaning that there are none left.)

iii)  *Situation*: in a restaurant – two friends talking
*Background noises*: restaurant
'Mmmmmmmm, this is absolutely . . . [delicious].' (Or any other appropriate positive adjective that collocates with food.)

iv)   *Situation*: formal business meeting
'On the one hand, I feel it might be a good idea to consider his proposal, but, on the other hand . . . [I think we need to consider the other proposals carefully too].' (Or any other appropriate variations.)

v) *Situation*: radio news broadcast
   *Background noises*: interference
   'The President of the United States of America announced today that he
   had no intention of reducing the number of . . . [nuclear weapons]
   located in Europe. The Prime Minister in her address to Parliament
   today said she fully . . . [agreed with his decision].'

The clues on the recording are:
i)   intonation, vocabulary ('exhausted', 'cup')
ii)  background noises, intonation, apology phrases
iii) background noises, intonation, vocabulary ('absolutely')
iv)  connectors ('on the one hand', 'on the other hand'), register
v)   register, knowledge of politics, vocabulary ('fully').

■■■■■■■

# Step 7   How do you organise your listening practice?

| Materials: | Learner's Book page 65 |
|---|---|
| Items to cover: | Suggestions. |
| Time: | 10 minutes |

Ask your learners to read the suggestions in the Learner's Book for
organising their listening practice and encourage an exchange of ideas.

**Further reading**

Brown, G. and Yule, G. 1983. This book examines the nature of spoken language
   and the principles and techniques for teaching spoken production and listening
   comprehension. It also deals with how to assess spoken language.
Hawkins, E. 1984. A description of the area of curriculum development known as
   'language awareness'. The final section shows how to conduct a brief course in
   'how to listen'.

*Recommended for learners*

Blundell, L and Stokes, J. 1981. This book aims to develop the listening skills of
   students who have had little exposure to authentic spoken English. Each recording

is accompanied by a task which encourages students to sift out the relevant information from what they hear. The Teacher's Book contains a complete tapescript and answers, making it useful for self-study.

British Council and Macmillan, 1984. A series of eight video cassettes that show realistic characters in everyday situations, speaking colloquial English. There are four levels from elementary to advanced and each cassette concentrates on key language functions.

Elsworth, S. 1982. This book provides realistic listening material to consolidate and practise the recognition and use of numbers in English. It includes tapescripts and answers.

Hughes, A. and Trudgill, P. 1979. An introductory survey of the main regional and social varieties of spoken British English. The accompanying cassette contains edited interviews with transcriptions in the book.

McDowell, J. and Hart, C. 1987. (See page 35.)

Mortimer, C. 1985. This book contains practice activities which concentrate on stress time, weak forms, contractions, consonant clusters and linking words.

St Clair Stokes, J. 1984. The approach in this book is similar to that in Blundell and Stokes (1981).

# 2.4 Speaking

■ □ □ □ □ □ □

## Step 1   How do you feel about speaking English?

| | |
|---|---|
| Materials: | Learner's Book pages 66–67 |
| Items to cover: | Learners' attitudes towards speaking English can affect the way they learn. |
| Time: | 15 minutes |

1. Lead a class discussion about the attitudes presented in the Learner's Book. Elicit or suggest the following points:

   *Herbert* is typical of the 'analytic' type (see 1.2). He is so concerned with being correct that his spoken English becomes hesitant and laborious.

   *Purificacion* is typical of the 'relaxed' type. She is more concerned with fluency than accuracy and is probably easily satisfied with her language achievements (see 1.2).

   *Maria Elena* feels, as many people do, that her personality changes when she speaks a foreign language. This may be because one's tone of voice often does change. For some people this can be inhibiting, for others, motivating.

   *Vladimir* is unrealistic about the standard of pronunciation he can achieve. Everybody has a different level of satisfaction; it is important for learners to know their own and decide whether this is realistic or not in terms of their aims.

   *Valérie* reflects the view of many learners who have very definite ideas about 'correct English', often without considering why they feel this way.

2. and 3. Ask your learners to think about their own attitudes towards speaking English and discuss these in class. Encourage them to consider what effect these attitudes may have on their speaking.

■ ■ □ □ □ □ □

# Step 2   What do you know about speaking English?

| | |
|---|---|
| Materials: | Learner's Book pages 67–71 |
| | Cassette |
| Items to cover: | 1. *English as a world language* |
| | 2. *Pronunciation* |
| | 3. *Stress* |
| | Syllables |
| | Words in sentences |
| | 4. *Intonation* |
| | 5. *Features of spoken English* |
| | Differences between written and spoken English. |
| | Factors influencing choice of language, levels of |
| | formality. |
| Time: | 1 hour 35 minutes |

## 1   English as a world language

The aim of points (a), (b) and (c) is to widen the learners' perspective, as they often have a limited view of English as a world language.

**Answers**

a) i)   320,000,000 approximately
   ii)  390,000,000 approximately
   Your class may also be interested to know about other major world languages: it is estimated that Chinese is spoken as a first language by 900,000,000 and by 920,000,000 as a second language; Spanish is spoken as a first language by 210,000,000 and by 250,000,000 as a second language; Hindi by 180,000,000 as a first language, and Russian by 145,000,000 as a first language and by 270,000,000 as a second language. (Source: *Language Monthly,* No. 18 March, 1985.)

b) English is the principal language of the United States, Canada, Great Britain, Ireland, Australia, New Zealand and of such countries as the Bahamas, Jamaica, Barbados, Grenada, Trinidad and Tobago, St Lucia, Belize and Guyana. It is the official language of more than a dozen African countries, as well as of various British dependencies such as Gibraltar, Hong Kong, and numerous islands in the Caribbean, and the Atlantic, Indian, and Pacific oceans. In India it has the title of 'associate official language' and is generally used in conversation between people from different parts of the country. In dozens of other countries throughout the world it is the unofficial second language. (Source: Katzner, *The Languages of the World*, Routledge & Kegan Paul, 1986.)

c) 1. Nigerian English    4. Irish English
   2. 'English' English    5. US English
   3. Australian English   6. Indian English

**Tapescript**

*Accent 1*

I'm the fourth in a family of four, of um . . . of 13 I'm the fourth in that family. Um . . . ten of us are alive and we hold different positions: company manager, lecturer, businessman, television broadcaster, um . . . secondary school teachers. I got married in 198 . . . 1973. I have four children, the first three are boys um . . . and the fourth a girl. The first and second boy are in secondary school, um . . . the third child, the boy, is in Primary 5, and the last, the girl, who'll be five on the 31st of this month, is er . . . in Primary 1.

*Accent 2*

I'm married and I've got three children, two boys and a girl. The boys are 21 and 19 and the girl is nine, so it's quite a big gap. The older boy is doing a B.Ed. at the moment at um . . . a Poly, and he's hoping to teach. The next boy is working in a greengrocer's because he doesn't really know what he wants to do, but he'll eventually make up his mind, I'm sure. And the little girl who's . . . who, as I say, is nine – she's still at school, of course – and interested in swimming and ballet, and 'My Fair Lady' at the moment, which she sings constantly.

*Accent 3*

I have two sisters, one's called Judith and one's called Jane. Jane is a teacher, and my sister Judith has two children and she works for my father in a shop. I have no brothers. Um . . . my sisters and I all went to the same school and we enjoy swimming and dancing and going to parties and things like that.

*Accent 4*

My family's quite small, really. I've got um . . . no grandparents, they're all dead. Er . . . My parents are still alive and I have a sister and two brothers. My sister is married and she has five boys, so we're all a bit disappointed about that because we'd like a girl. I'm not married myself, so maybe it's my duty to get married and have some girls.

*Accent 5*

Well, there's my mum and my dad, and they run a gas station. And my mum's called Maddy and she's 48, and my dad's called Sid and he's 51. And then there's my kid sister Sally. She's a freshman in college. And my baby brother Scott. And he's still in high school.

*Accent 6*

I belong to a very small family. My parents er . . . have two children, myself and a brother, who's working as a chartered accountant in a bank. And I'm a schoolteacher and my immediate family is also a very small family. I have two sons, one is 11 years old and another is five. And all the three of us go to the same school. And my husband is er . . . in a government office . . . it's called National Building Construction Corporation. And er . . . my brother lives in the same town as I do and we meet pretty often. And my parents live with my brother — it's a kind of joint family — and er . . . we visit each other pretty often. And my husband's family consists . . . right now it consists of a brother and a sister and who also live very close by. And all of us, you know my brother and my husband's brother and sister, all of us have two children each, both couples.

d) This section encourages learners to consider the type of English they want to speak and the factors which have contributed to this decision.

## 2 Pronunciation

This helps learners become more aware of the typical pronunciation problems that speakers of their language have when speaking English, thus giving them a basis for self-assessment activities in Step 3. Try to elicit the problems from your learners but also be prepared to guide them. Useful sources of information are the 'List of likely errors' in Baker (1982b:138–55) and Swan and Smith (1987).

## 3 Stress

*Syllables*

Point out to your learners that wrongly stressed syllables can lead to misunderstanding. Refer them to the examples in their books and play the cassette.

a) Ask your learners to mark the stressed syllables using whatever notation system they are familiar with.

**Answers**

   ■       ■         ■             ■              ■

banana   area   photograph   photographer   advertisement

b) Play the cassette again to demonstrate the pronunciation of the words, in particular the unstressed syllables.

c) Play the cassette again and ask the learners to repeat the words to practise where to put the stress.

Make sure your learners know how to use dictionaries to find information about stress.

*Words in sentences*

This is a practice activity designed to encourage learners to use stress variations. In real life, one would, of course, use short answers to the questions. Point out to your learners that while this exercise may not produce natural discourse, its purpose is to demonstrate the mechanics of stress and to give practice in this.

Play the two example sentences on the cassette, making sure that the class understand the difference between them. Then ask learners to practise asking and answering questions about the model sentence in pairs.

**Tapescript and answers**

i)   Who gave Jackie the bicycle?
     *David* gave Jackie the bicycle.

ii)  How did Jackie get the bicycle?
     David *gave* Jackie the bicycle.

iii) Who did David give the bicycle to?
     David gave *Jackie* the bicycle.

iv)  Which present did David give Jackie?
     David gave Jackie the *bicycle*.

This exercise has been recorded by native speakers on the cassette. Play it afterwards for the learners to listen to and repeat, if necessary.

## 4   Intonation

Intonation patterns in English can be very varied and subtle. There are several books available with relevant information (see pages 125–6). The aim of this section is to make two points:
– intonation can indicate what the speaker means
– intonation can indicate how the speaker feels.
Play the example on the cassette to the learners (books closed) and discuss the meaning. Then play the three short conversations and ask what the second speaker means or how he or she feels each time (see tapescript).

**Answers**

i)   means 'I apologise for stepping on your foot.'
ii)  means 'Yes, good idea, let's go.'
iii) means 'Not again, I don't really want to, but I will if I have to.'

You might feel it is appropriate to ask your learners to mark the intonation as they listen, using whatever notation system they are familiar with. It could also be helpful for learners to copy the examples of intonation from the cassette.

**Tapescript**

i)  A: Ow! My foot!

    B: Oh sorry!

ii) A: Let's go to the cinema.

    B: Oh all right!

iii) A: Let's go to the cinema.

    B: Oh all right.

## 5 Features of spoken English

a) The aim of this exercise is to make learners aware of some of the differences between written and spoken English. Many learners do not appreciate these differences and think that the written form is the one they should use when speaking. This exercise draws the learners' attention to some of the features of natural English, as spoken by native speakers; these include unfinished sentences, hesitation techniques and contractions.

   Ask your learners whether they have noticed any differences between the two forms and, if so, let them give examples. Then ask the class to consider the features of the written and recorded invitations and to complete the chart. Possible features include:

| *Written* | *Spoken* |
|---|---|
| formal | informal |
| abbreviations | repetition |
| brief | longer |
| punctuation | interrupted sentences |
| layout | false starts |
| | unfinished sentences |
| | contractions |
| | intonation |
| | hesitation |

**Tapescript**

*Wayne*: Hello?
*Tracey*: Wayne?
*Wayne*: Yes?
*Tracey*: It's Tracey here.
*Wayne*: Hello Tracey. How are you?
*Tracey*: Fine. How are you?
*Wayne*: Yeah. Very well thank you. Haven't heard from you for some time.

*Tracey*: Oh no, um . . . I I was just ringing to invite you to a party.
*Wayne*: Oh right.
*Tracey*: Er, Now, um, it's on 24th September, that's a Saturday.
*Wayne*: Saturday, is that . . . is that next Saturday?
*Tracey*: No, no, it's the next Saturday, the one after.
*Wayne*: Right, OK.
*Tracey*: Hm, about eight o'clock. [Yeah]. Um, all the gang'll be there. [Oh good]. Er, it's my birthday, actually.
*Wayne*: Oh really.
*Tracey*: Yeah, anyway um, it's at my house. Er, um, my mum and dad are going out.
*Wayne*: Yeah. Oh good, that means we can make as much noise . . .
*Tracey*: Yeah. So, that's number 91, remember?
*Wayne*: Yeah, what's the name of your road again?
*Tracey*: Gade Street. That's GADE.
*Wayne*: Gade Street and er, you said 21?
*Tracey*: No, no, 91.
*Wayne*: 91 [Yeah] Gade Street. [Yes] Right, OK. Yes, that's OK.
*Tracey*: Right, see you then.
*Wayne*: Great. Look forward to seeing you.
*Tracey*: Right then. Thanks Wayne. Bye.

b) This section aims to help learners become familiar with the concept of register. Many other teaching materials, such as Jones (1981) include similar information. It contains information which they should find useful when completing the task in (c).

c) Allow time for discussion of the answers after each conversation.

**Tapescript**

*Conversation 1*

*Mr Bradley*: Come in. Ah, Debbie, what can I do for you?     •
*Debbie*: Um . . . here you are Mr Bradley. I'm terribly sorry I've just found the Poiser file that I'd mislaid.
*Mr Bradley*: That's taken rather a long time, hasn't it?
*Debbie*: Um . . . well actually I, I lost it, and I found it again, it was um under a heap of letters on my desk.
*Mr Bradley*: I really think you should be a bit more careful about where you file things in the future. OK give it to me.
*Debbie*: So sorry, I thought I'd put it in the filing cabinet.
*Mr Bradley*: Yes, yes, yes, all right, thank you. Don't do it again.

*Conversation 2*

*Mother*: Come along now Jilly love, eat up your dinner.
*Jilly*: No, I don't want to, I don't like it, . . . hate mashed potato.
*Mother*: You don't hate mashed potato, and even if you do, you've got to eat at least some of it.
*Jilly*: I don't want it and I'm not going to eat it.
*Mother*: If you don't eat it, you won't go to Granny's on Saturday.

*Jilly*: I don't care, I just don't want to eat it.
*Mother*: You will eat it and do as you are told.
*Jilly*: No!

*Conversation 3*

A: It's er . . . [Mm?] it's a bit warm in here isn't it? Um, do you mind if I open the window?
B: Yeah!
A: Er . . . well we we we've we've got the radiator on, er, do you mind if, I mean . . . er just half an inch.
B: Look, I'm here because I've got a stiff neck because I sat next door to an open window all yesterday.
A: Well, listen. Why why don't we swap swap places?
B: Oh blimey, one pain in the neck is enough for a day.
A: And you could sit next to the radiator and then I . . .
B: I said no!
A: Ah!

**Answers**

|  | *Conversation 1* | *Conversation 2* | *Conversation 3* |
|---|---|---|---|
| What is the relationship between the speakers? | Employee to boss | Parent to child | Two strangers |
| Where are they? | In the office | At home | In a waiting room |
| What is the topic? | The Poiser file | Dinner | The window |
| What are their reasons for speaking? | giving information about location of file, apologising | ordering child to eat dinner | asking permission/ making a request |
| How do they feel? | apologetic/ worried/irritated | angry/stubborn | rude/unfriendly unsociable |

d) Ask your learners to list as many ways of asking somebody to be quiet as they can. Elicit examples and arrange them on the board or overhead projector, according to register, starting with the most formal and finishing with the most informal. You may need to give them some ideas to start them off, for example:
   – I wonder if you could possibly be a little quieter please?
   – Could you be a little quieter please?
   – Be quiet please!
   – Do be quiet!
   – Shut up!

■ ■ ■ ☐ ☐ ☐ ☐

# Step 3   How well are you doing?

| | |
|---|---|
| Materials: | Learner's Book pages 72–75<br>Cassette<br>Information about relevant examinations<br>Selection of photographs/pictures<br>Cassette recorder(s) and blank cassettes |
| Items to cover: | *1. Points to assess*<br>Focus on accuracy<br>Focus on fluency<br>Activity: Describing a photograph<br>Activity: Recording yourself<br>*2. Test yourself in a practice activity*<br>*3. Assess your performance in a real-life situation*<br>*4. Examples* |
| Time: | 55 minutes when you introduce self-assessment in this skill for the first time. Thereafter, 5–10 minute sessions when necessary. |

If you are doing a Step 3 for the first time, read pages 65–7 in *2.1 Extending vocabulary*. If your learners are doing a Step 3 for the first time, refer them to page 30 in *2.1 Extending vocabulary* in the Learner's Book.

## 1   Points to assess

Speaking is one of the skills that concerns learners most. The assessment of it involves many different aspects and learners often need training in order to be aware of the points to assess and to know how to select these themselves. We have therefore provided detailed information for learners in this section and they will need careful guidance from you when studying it.

Check that your learners understand the difference beween accuracy and fluency (see 1.1(2)) and go through the lists of points. If your learners are working towards an examination, you could adapt the lists according to the requirements of the exam. Make sure you and your learners are familiar with these. Such information is readily available from Examination Boards and Guides.

## Focus on accuracy

The suggested list is intended to be fairly detailed but, at the same time, accessible to learners, although you should check that they understand the metalanguage. The points may be adapted and added to as desired.

## Focus on fluency

These are less easy to define and we have chosen to focus on just two areas:
a)  getting meaning across successfully
b)  being able to speak spontaneously without long pauses and repetitious hesitations, such as 'er . . . er . . . um . . . er . . .'

### Activity: Describing a photograph

This activity gives learners practice in assessment and aims to prepare them for assessing themselves (see the activity which follows). The cassette contains recordings of two Spanish learners describing the photograph.

**Tapescript**

*Learner A*

In this picture I can . . . I can see um some people . . . er . . . they are celebrating a wedding. Um . . . they they are celebrating the wedding with champagne . . . I I don't know . . . *Cava*. Um . . . I . . . they look happy um . . . everybody's smi . . . smi . . . smiling. Um . . . they they look pretty dresses because er . . . a wedding . . . er . . . I don't know er what more to say about it.

*Learner B*

A couple . . . I can see a couple . . . er um has been got married er and they are in front of the Church. Er the woman has got in the right hand a bouquet and in the left er er . . . a cup. I think they are going to drink champagne. Er er there er . . . there there are another there is another woman – I think is the mother of the of the girl who is going er who has been got married. Um . . . er . . . the man has got in the right hand er gloves and a hat. Er . . . he's very smart. Um . . . in the left hand a cup. All of them are going to drink champagne. Another man is going to take er . . . a photo. I think er somebody has taken a photo.

### Activity: Recording yourself

Since the criteria involved in assessing speaking can be very specific and numerous, we suggest the following classroom practice activity. The first time your learners do it, it also serves a diagnostic function as they go through the lists to find out which points they need to select and work on for further self-assessment.

a) Bring into class as many cassette recorders as you can, a supply of blank cassettes and a number of interesting photos or pictures for your learners to talk about. Give each learner a different picture and ask them to work in pairs. Learner A is recorded talking to Learner B about his or her photo for about a minute; then it is the turn of Learner B. If the recording is done outside the classroom by learners working individually, remind them to have a particular person in mind when talking about the picture. This will probably affect the way they speak.

b) Ask learners to listen to their recordings and try to assess their spoken English by referring to the lists of points to assess and deciding whether they are satisfied or not.

c) At this stage, it can be useful for learners to discuss their assessment with another learner or with you. This discussion activity provides learners who have had little practice in self-assessment with valuable training and confidence building.

*Note:* If tape recorders are not available, learners can assess each other in pairs.

## 2   Test yourself in a practice activity

Ask the class to read Jürgen's strategy for testing his pronunciation and stress. Elicit other ideas from your learners and discuss these with the class. Encourage the learners to test themselves regularly and suggest materials which they might find helpful (see pages 125–6).

## 3   Assess your performance in a real-life situation

Santiago gives a practical example of how you can assess yourself in conversation. (He refers to *Just a Minute!* which is a confidence-building activity you will find in Step 6.) See if your learners have tried anything similar and ask what they learnt from it.

## 4   Examples

In order to give your learners an example of how to use the self-assessment chart, ask them to look at those filled in by Jürgen and Santiago. Encourage your learners to keep records of their progress.

■ ■ ■ ■ □ □ □

# Step 4   What do you need to do next?

| | |
|---|---|
| Materials: | Learner's Book page 75 |
| Items to cover: | Examples of learners' short-term aims. |
| Time: | 15–20 minutes when you introduce setting short-term aims in this skill for the first time. Thereafter, 5–10 minute sessions when necessary. |

If you are doing a Step 4 for the first time, read pages 67–8 in *2.1 Extending vocabulary*. If your learners are doing a Step 4 for the first time, refer them to page 32 in *2.1 Extending vocabulary* in the Learner's Book. They should then look at the examples of how Jürgen and Santiago set themselves short-term aims.

■ ■ ■ ■ ■ □ □

# Step 5   How do you prefer to practise your speaking?

| | |
|---|---|
| Materials: | Learner's Book pages 76–77<br>Cassette |
| Items to cover: | 1. *Personal strategies*<br>2. *Time to experiment*<br>   Activity: Problem solving<br>3. *Choose a new strategy* |
| Time: | 30 minutes |

## 1   Personal strategies

Check that your learners understand the strategies described. Elicit from them what they do and encourage an exchange of information.

Learners not living in an English-speaking country may need to use ingenuity to find enough opportunities for practising speaking in a real-life situation. The learners here demonstrate how they have overcome this problem. Alphonsine's strategy, although she may not be speaking aloud, nevertheless gives practice in using English actively and is a good method of building up confidence for the real situation.

## 2  Time to experiment

*Activity: Problem solving*

Before playing the recording of Gail talking about her 'telephone strategy' for practising her spoken French, ask your learners to think about the kinds of problems they might have when speaking a foreign language on the telephone, for example, not being able to see the speaker, pressure of time or cost, not knowing specific 'telephone phrases' like 'Hang on', 'I'll transfer you'. Ask them if they can think of any ways they could improve their telephone techniques.

a) Ask your learners to look at the words that Gail uses and see if they can work out what her telephone strategy is.
b) Play the recording, twice if necessary.

**Tapescript**

I often have to speak French on the telephone for my job. I decided I needed to improve my telephone French as I often get stuck and I find this very frustrating. So this is why I devised what I call my 'telephone strategy'.

It's very simple really. I set up a cassette recorder next to my telephone on my desk and whenever I have to use French on the phone I just press the record button and record my half of the conversation. I then have a recording of what I actually said – or of what I should have said! Later, when I have a spare moment, I listen to my half of the conversation and I can usually hear where my problems really are.

At first it was a bit depressing, I sounded worse than I thought I was! But this made me even more determined to practise so I could improve. Often I can correct my own mistakes. Sometimes it's a question of not knowing the right expression like telling someone to hang on or to ring back later or that I'm going to transfer them. Sometimes it's vocabulary and often I hesitate because I'm not sure about the gender of a word, whether it's 'le' or 'la'. I also realised I was making very English hesitation sounds, like 'um' or 'er' so now I try to make French sounding hesitation noises like 'euh, ben'. Sometimes I ask a native speaker of French for help and ask them how they would say something. Then I re-record the bits I have problems with to give myself lots of practice and then I wait for the next opportunity to use them on the telephone. I try to use my telephone strategy whenever I can, but you have to be organised to do it and allow yourself the time. It's not always easy if you're really busy.

The other day I found an old cassette and listened to it – I've made some progress thank goodness!

c) Encourage the class to discuss how useful this strategy would be for them.

### 3   Choose a new strategy

Encourage your learners to experiment with new strategies for practising their speaking in order to help them find the one(s) they prefer.

────   ■ ■ ■ ■ ■ □   ────

# Step 6   Do you need to build up your confidence?

| | |
|---|---|
| Materials: | Learner's Book pages 77–79<br>Cassette<br>Topic cards<br>Cassette recorder and blank cassette (optional) |
| Items to cover: | 1. *Thinking-time techniques*<br>    Activity: Just a Minute!<br>2. *Suggestions* |
| Time: | 30–40 minutes |

### 1   Thinking-time techniques

a)  Ask your learners to read about Dominique's experience. Find out if they have ever been in a situation like this and what they did.

Dominique's comments reflect the typical anxiety about how to deal with tricky situations when speaking a foreign language. In such situations 'Thinking-time' techniques help learners to build up their confidence and, as a result, feel more able to cope and react spontaneously in English.

b)  Play the cassette to demonstrate how 'Thinking-time' techniques can be used to avoid silences and to give the impression that the speaker is in control when answering a difficult question. Ask your learners to note down any other phrases which they would be able to use in a similar situation.

Here are some possible examples if your learners are short of ideas:
'Honestly . . . '
'You know . . . '
'You know what I think, I think . . . '
'All things considered, I must say . . . '
'The thing is . . . '
Rhetorical questions such as: 'Yes, what is the Prime Minister's foreign policy decision all about?'
For further examples see Jones (1981:25–7).

**Tapescript**

*Interviewer*:  If I could just turn to you now, er . . . Ms Sinclair, what do you think about the Prime Minister's latest foreign policy decisions?

*Ms Sinclair*:  Ah yes, now what do I think about the Prime Minister's latest foreign policy decisions? Well, actually, that's a very interesting question and it's one I've been thinking about for some time.
   You see, it's like this, er, how shall I put it? Well, as far as I can see, er to my mind, what the Prime Minister has actually done here . . .

c) Give the class five minutes to choose and practise the phrases from (b) so that they are ready to move on to the activity without having to refer to their books. Encourage them to be realistic about what they can learn in the time.

   Tell your learners that although the use of 'er . . . ' and 'um . . . ' is natural in spoken English, overuse will produce a boring and repetitive style. Remind them also of the oral communication strategies practised in *2.1 Extending vocabulary* Step 6.

### Activity: Just a Minute!

Tell the class that this is a fluency exercise and you will not be concerned with their mistakes.

Produce a set of topic cards; each card should have one topic clearly written on it. Your choice of topics will depend on the level and interests of your class. Have some easy ones to start with, for example, breakfast, trees, pets, Italian food. Use these easy cards to help your learners become familiar with the activity. Make sure you also have some more difficult topics: the more obscure or strange the topic, for example, the life cycle of the lesser spotted toad, Chinese restaurants in New York, the economic development of the Falkland Islands, the more the learners will have to use 'Thinking-time' techniques.

Play the cassette in order to demonstrate the game to your learners. In the extract, Paz from Spain, who is living in a student hostel in London, talks about English food and Chen from China about Chinese restaurants in New York.

Choose a learner and give him or her a card. The learner chosen should try to speak for one minute on the topic on the card using whatever 'Thinking-time' techniques he or she wishes. Do not allow any time for preparation. Ask the others in the class what 'Thinking-time' techniques were used.

It can be very useful to record some of the learners doing this. Encourage them to practise on their own and, if they wish, to record themselves and listen afterwards.

If your class is large, or your learners nervous about speaking in front of each other, the activity can be done in pairs. Give each learner a card; A should speak about the topic on B's card and vice versa.

**Tapescript**

*Paz*

My topic is English food. I really hate English food, I mean, I think it's dreadful, I mean, compared with the food of my country. I'm really . . . I'm really having a really bad time, I mean, I mean, with this er . . . eating English food. I don't know . . . I mean . . . er I don't know what is the the problem of this English food but er . . . I mean, I think they overcook vegetables. I mean they, I mean they they um . . . I don't kn . . . I mean, fish! Er we don't hardly eat any fish. I don't know why. I mean these people don't eat fish and and it's er . . . an it's an island. I mean er I mean er they they they eat er . . . meat er . . . all most of the time and I mean the meat is is all so horrible and and they don't eat any any fruit. They they eat, I mean sweets, I mean, sweet things all the time. That makes you so fat, I mean, this is not healthy, this is not a very healthy kind of food. I don't know, I mean, I don't know what is the problem. They don't have a cuisine, I mean, like the other countries, I mean, it's er . . . I mean . . .
[Well done! Well done!]
[You really hate English food, don't you?]
I do!

*Chen*

Chinese restaurant in New York. Um . . . I've never been to New York, but I think Chinese restaurant in New York would be not like Chinese restaurant at all. It would be like New York restaurant, actually because I think you have to fit into the New York people's taste to attract customers. It must be a lot of quick food because New Yorkers um would like to go to work as soon as they finish their lunch or supper anything — so it will be er . . . very quick and . . . what else? Let me think . . . it must be they must be cheap because lots of people um er like to have cheap food and they think Chinese food are good and it must be have a good quality . . . so New York foo . . . Chinese restaurant in New York food . . . I well . . . well . . . Chinese Chinese restaurant in New York must be good, cheap and easy to make and . . . what else?

## 2  Suggestions

Refer the learners to the suggestions in the Learner's Book for building up their confidence and check that they understand them.

■ ■ ■ ■ ■ ■ ■

# Step 7   How do you organise your speaking practice?

| | |
|---|---|
| Materials: | Learner's Book page 79 |
| Items to cover: | Suggestions. |
| Time: | 15 minutes |

Ask your learners to look at the suggestions in the Learner's Book for organising their speaking practice and encourage an exchange of ideas.

**Further reading**

Baker, A. 1981. An intermediate pronunciation course which aims to train students to recognise and produce English sounds, and includes work on stress and intonation.
Baker, A. 1982a. An elementary pronunciation course which provides practice in the pronunciation of English sounds, word stress and intonation.
Baker, A. 1982b. A Teacher's Guide to the above two books. It also contains a chapter which lists the errors likely to be made by students of different mother tongues and, for students not mentioned in this list, a diagnostic pronunciation test is included.
Bradford, B. 1988. This book aims to make learners aware of the main features of intonation and contains activities for both controlled and freer practice in a range of conversational situations.
Brazil, D. et al. 1980. This book describes the interactive significance of intonation, relates it to an existing description of discourse structure and discusses both the general question of the place of intonation in language teaching and how this particular description might be taught.
Brown, G. and Yule, G. 1983. (See page 107.)
Ferris, D. 1983. A description of five types of activities used for training second language learners of English in self-assessment of their oral communication skills.
Swan, M. 1980. (See page 53.)

*Recommended for learners*

Baker, A. 1981, 1982a, 1982b. (See *Further reading*.)
Fitzpatrick, A. 1987. A book designed to help students who need to improve their spoken English in the context of conferences and congresses. Can be used for self-study.

Jones, L. 1981. This book contains a variety of exercises and activities to help students increase their confidence and improve their accuracy in conversation.
Mortimer, C. 1985. (See page 108.)
Ockenden, M. 1983. Short dialogues and exercises in 'small talk' for students who need to become familiar with this kind of informal English and to have practice in this social skill. Can be used for self-study.

# 2.5 Reading

■ □ □ □ □ □ □

## Step 1    How do you feel about reading English?

| Materials: | Learner's Book pages 80–81 |
|---|---|
| Items to cover: | Learners' attitudes towards reading English can affect the way they learn. |
| Time: | 15 minutes |

1. Ask your learners to consider the attitudes presented in the Learner's Book. Lead a class discussion and elicit or suggest the following points:

   *Roger* may not enjoy reading in any language very much and may resent having to read at work – especially in a foreign language. His negative attitude to reading may be carried over into a language learning situation. Learners like Roger need a lot of guidance in order to become aware that reading can be pleasurable and can help language acquisition. They should be encouraged to read materials about subjects they are interested in.

   *Susanne* has only one strategy for reading English, which she equates with learning words and finds hard work. This is probably due to the way she has been taught to approach English texts in the classroom. Learners like Susanne need to be more careful to select reading materials at a suitable level of difficulty, on topics which interest them. They will also need to be made aware of other reading strategies.

   *Gilbert* is one of those people who loves reading and pursues his own interests in other languages too. Recent research seems to indicate that reading is a vastly underrated source of input for language acquisition. (Krashen, TESOL, New York, 1985.)

2. and 3. Ask your learners to think about their own attitudes towards

127

reading English and to discuss these in class. Encourage them to consider what effect these attitudes may have on their reading.

———— ■ ■ ☐ ☐ ☐ ☐ ☐ ————

# Step 2   What do you know about reading English?

| Materials: | Learner's Book pages 81–83<br>Examples of different text types: newspapers, telephone directory, learners' magazines, etc. (optional) |
|---|---|
| Items to cover: | 1. *Reading speed*<br>2. *Reading strategies*<br>  Skimming, scanning, reading for detail.<br>  Activity: Reading a menu |
| Time: | 35–40 minutes |

## 1   Reading speed

a) Encourage your class to be as specific as they can about their reading problems in English.

b) It is an interesting exercise for learners to consider how they read in their own language. If their language has a linear script they will probably come to the conclusion that they read in chunks of about five centimetres (three or four words) rather than stopping to look at every word.

c) Ask the learners to try the 'test'.

d) Make sure that your learners think about the advantages of reading in chunks *before* reading the text. You will probably find it helpful to discuss the text with your class to see how much they understand and agree with.

## 2   Reading strategies

The aim of this section is to make learners become aware of different reading strategies: skimming, scanning, reading for detail. Go through the different strategies with your class and ask them to think about possible situations where they might use these. You could bring examples of different text types into the classroom, for example, newspapers, a telephone directory, learners' magazines, in order to demonstrate the strategies.

Very often learners only read in English to pick up new language. We feel this is a very valid reason, but it should not prevent them from using the other strategies where appropriate. We suggest you recommend to your learners that reading for language should come *after* reading for meaning.

### Activity: Reading a menu

**Possible answers**

Your learners could use a variety of strategies depending on their reason for reading the menu.

*Skimming*: if you were not sure what you wanted to eat and wanted to get an overall idea of what was on offer.

*Scanning:* if you went into the restaurant with a specific idea of what you wanted to eat, e.g. fish, and you checked the menu quickly for the fish section.

*Reading for detail*: if you wanted to try something you have not had before, and you read the menu carefully to find out exactly what was in the dish and how it was cooked.

The aim of the layout question is to help learners become aware of features such as headings and print size as clues to meaning and aids to prediction. Ask learners how the layout of the menu helped them with their reading strategy.

If you feel it would be appropriate for your learners, you could take into class newspapers in different languages and scripts, for example, Chinese, Arabic, Russian, and ask learners to identify different text types, for example, articles about sport, TV programmes and politics. This activity should demonstrate how much information can be obtained from such layout features as titles, headlines, diagrams and photos.

■ ■ ■ □ □ □ □

# Step 3   How well are you doing?

| Materials: | Learner's Book pages 84–85 |
|---|---|
| Items to cover: | 1. *Points to assess*<br>2. *Test yourself in a practice activity*<br>3. *Assess your performance in a real-life situation*<br>4. *Examples* |
| Time: | 15–20 minutes when you introduce self-assessment in this skill for the first time. Thereafter, 5–10 minute sessions when necessary. |

If you are doing a Step 3 for the first time, read pages 65–7 in *2.1 Extending vocabulary*. If your learners are doing a Step 3 for the first time, refer them to page 30 in *2.1 Extending vocabulary* in the Learner's Book.

### 1   Points to assess

To help learners assess their reading comprehension, point out that they should be clear about both their reason for reading and the type of text.

### 2   Test yourself in a practice activity

Ask your learners to read Erik's suggestion and elicit other ideas from the class. Encourage the learners to test themselves regularly.

### 3   Assess your performance in a real-life situation

Refer your learners to Sofia's comments. Ask them to think of a real-life situation they have been in recently and to assess their performance.

### 4   Examples

In order to give your learners an example of how to use the self-assessment chart, ask them to look at those filled in by Erik and Sofia. Encourage your learners to keep records of their progress.

■ ■ ■ ■ □ □ □

# Step 4   What do you need to do next?

| | |
|---|---|
| Materials: | Learner's Book page 86 |
| Items to cover: | Examples of learners' short-term aims. |
| Time: | 15–20 minutes when you introduce setting short-term aims in this skill for the first time. Thereafter, 5–10 minute sessions when necessary. |

If you are doing a Step 4 for the first time, read pages 67–8 in *2.1 Extending vocabulary*. If your learners are doing a Step 4 for the first time, refer them to page 32 in *2.1 Extending vocabulary* in the Learner's Book. They should then look at the examples of how Erik and Sofia set themselves short-term aims.

■ ■ ■ ■ ■ □ □

# Step 5   How do you prefer to practise your reading?

| | |
|---|---|
| Materials: | Learner's Book pages 87–88 |
| Items to cover: | *1. Personal strategies*<br>*2. Suggestions*<br>*3. Choose a new strategy* |
| Time: | 20 minutes |

### 1   Personal strategies

Check that your learners understand the strategies described. Elicit from them what they do and encourage an exchange of ideas.

### 2   Suggestions

Direct the learners to the list of suggestions in their books and check that they understand them.

### 3   Choose a new strategy

Encourage your learners to experiment with new strategies for practising their reading in order to help them find the one(s) they prefer.

---

■ ■ ■ ■ ■ □

# Step 6   Do you need to build up your confidence?

| | |
|---|---|
| Materials: | Learner's Book pages 88–90 |
| Items to cover: | 1. *Predicting* <br> Activity: Completing sentences <br> 2. *Guessing unknown words* <br> Activity: Guessing out of context <br> Activity: Guessing in context <br> Activity: Discover the useful tip |
| Time: | 35 minutes |

### 1   Predicting

Ask your learners to read about predicting in their books and to try the 'test'.

*Activity: Completing sentences*

Ask the class to complete the sentences and compare ideas. Discuss with them what helped them guess.

**Answers**

a) raspberries, peaches. (Or any other summer fruits.)
b) but showers later in the South West. (Or other appropriate information about the weather.)
c) couldn't help admiring him as a surgeon. (Or doctor, registrar, etc.)

### 2   Guessing unknown words

If we are faced with an unknown word while reading a text in our own language, we first decide whether we really need or want to understand the word. If not, the usual strategy is to skip it. If we think the word is important for understanding the text we usually hypothesise about its meaning. It is unusual to go straight to the dictionary whenever we see an unknown word, but learners do this frequently in a foreign language, thus interrupting their reading. This might be good for their vocabulary development, but it does not improve their reading skills or encourage them to rely on themselves. Suggest to your learners that they use dictionaries to check their guesses *after* they have finished reading the whole text, if it is a short one, and, if it is a long text, after they have finished reading a sizeable chunk.

Go through the 'clues' in the Learner's Book, giving examples where necessary. Further examples are provided in Underhill (1980:37) and in Davies and Whitney (1984).

### Activity: Guessing out of context

After the learners have discussed what they think the meanings of the four words might be, ask them to compare their ideas and to say what features of the words enabled them to make their guesses. Do not confirm the correct meanings yet.

### Activity: Guessing in context

The class should find guessing the words in context more meaningful and considerably easier. Confirm the correct meanings. Ask learners which clues helped them guess and which of the two activities was the more useful.

### Activity: Discover the useful tip

If the learners are concerned about the validity of defining nonsense words, point out that they will be reinforcing and testing the strategy they learnt in the previous activity. (They need not guess the *exact* answers, but their words should fit the context, as in the example in the Learner's Book.)

**Answers**

1 reading
2 context
3 learning
4 dictionary
5 unsure

■ ■ ■ ■ ■ ■ ■

# Step 7   How do you organise your reading practice?

| | |
|---|---|
| Materials: | Learner's Book page 91 |
| Items to cover: | Suggestions. |
| Time: | 10 minutes |

Ask your learners to look at the suggestions in the Learner's Book for organising their speaking practice and encourage an exchange of ideas.

**Further reading**

Buzan, T. 1982. (See page 53.)
Davies, E. and Whitney, N. 1979, 1981, 1984. There are three books in this reading comprehension course, which aims to contextualise what is read, to build up an awareness of the different features of written English discourse, and to integrate reading as a language skill with the other skills of listening, speaking, writing and studying.
Grellet, F. 1981. This is a practical guide to reading comprehension exercises.
Hedge, T. 1985b. (See page 53.)
Nuttall, C. 1982. This book examines the various skills needed to read effectively and suggests classroom approaches and materials to develop and integrate these, as well as to integrate reading with other language skills.
Scott, M. et al. 1984. A report on a procedure devised to train students in efficient reading comprehension strategies, by using a 'standard exercise' which can be applied to almost any text.
Smith, F. 1978. (See page 78.)

*Recommended for learners*

Davies, E. and Whitney, N. 1979, 1981, 1984. (As above.)
Bell, J. et al. 1985. A workbook which aims to make authentic texts accessible to intermediate students of English by means of an extensive range of activities. A key to the exercises is included, making the materials suitable for self-study.

# 2.6 Writing

---

■ □ □ □ □ □ ──────────

## Step 1    How do you feel about writing English?

| | |
|---|---|
| Materials: | Learner's Book page 92 |
| Items to cover: | Learners' attitudes towards writing English can affect the way they learn. |
| Time: | 15 minutes |

1. Ask your learners to consider the attitudes presented in the Learner's Book. Lead a class discussion and elicit or suggest the following points:

   *Didier* does not feel secure in situations where he has to speak spontaneously because he is worried about making mistakes. He has more time to think when writing and therefore prefers to communicate in this way if he has the choice.

   *Bernhard* is typical of many learners who do not need to write in English, but do so only for the purpose of learning or practising new language.

   *Tanim* expresses the sentiments of many learners who have to master a new script in order to write English. He, however, has a positive attitude. In many multilingual classrooms there are some learners who are not aware of the extra difficulties of others in the class.

2. and 3. Ask your learners to think about their own attitudes towards writing English and to discuss these in class. Encourage them to consider what effect these attitudes may have on their writing.

■ ■ □ □ □ □

# Step 2   What do you know about writing English?

| Materials: | Learner's Book pages 93–96 |
|---|---|
| | Examples of text types (provided by learners or by you) |
| Items to cover: | 1. *What do people write?* |
| | Writing for communication; personal writing. |
| | 2. *Characteristics of written texts* |
| | Activity: Comparing written texts |
| | 3. *What are the features of a well-written text?* |
| | Activity: Detective work |
| Time: | 1 hour |

## 1   What do people write?

We have chosen to divide writing into the two broad categories of communication and personal use because:
– this takes into account the type of writing that learners of English spend a lot of time doing, such as noting down new words, taking notes in lessons in order to learn English, as well as writing to communicate with others;
– it makes it easier to select points for self-assessment.

Ask learners to add to the lists of types of writing on the diagram, if they can.

## 2   Characteristics of written texts

Remind your learners of the general differences between spoken and written English by referring them to *2.4 Speaking* Step 2.

### Activity: Comparing written texts

If your class are not able to find any suitable texts, be prepared to provide some yourself. Ask learners to compare the examples of writing brought into the class. The texts may be handwritten or typed, or they may be taken from published material. Ask your learners to look for characteristics which are specific to the different types of writing; some ideas can be found in the Learner's Book. The class should then make notes about their findings as suggested in their books; if they are competent writers in their language, they are probably already aware of most of the characteristics of written texts and will have many ideas of their own.

*Variation*:   You could select two or three examples of writing which you know are relevant to your learners' needs and focus on the characteristics of these. Select a variety of examples in order to encourage the class to compare and contrast, rather than focussing on only one type of written English. This will help provide a wider perspective, as well as a reason for discussion.

### 3   What are the features of a well-written text?

Draw your learners' attention to the information in their books. At this stage the features which they suggest will probably include such areas as grammar, vocabulary, spelling and punctuation.

*Activity: Detective work*

This activity is based on the technique of reformulation. For further details see Allwright (forthcoming).

When learners are comparing the two versions of the letter they should be noticing features such as style, organisation, and sequencing and linking devices.

■ ■ ■ □ □ □ □

# Step 3   How well are you doing?

| Materials: | Learner's Book pages 97–99 |
|---|---|
| Items to cover: | 1. *Points to assess*<br>Invent your own marking scheme<br>Activity: Marking an essay<br>2. *Test yourself in a practice activity*<br>3. *Assess your performance in a real-life situation*<br>4. *Examples* |
| Time: | 40 minutes when you introduce self-assessment in this skill for the first time. Thereafter, 5–10 minute sessions when necessary. |

If you are doing a Step 3 for the first time, read pages 65–7 in *2.1 Extending vocabulary*. If your learners are doing a Step 3 for the first time, refer them to page 30 in *2.1 Extending vocabulary* in the Learner's Book.

## 1 Points to assess

Refer your learners back to the list of features of a well-written text they drew up in Step 2(3) to remind them of points to assess in their writing. In addition, they need to be aware that:
- native-speaker readers have very high expectations concerning written texts, which should therefore be correct, coherent and presented in an appropriate style;
- as learners therefore need to be especially critical of their writing, more so than of other skills, their self-assessment will probably need to be more detailed and based on a wider range of points;
- for most situations where learners need to write English, they have the time and opportunity to draft, reflect and check, etc.; this means that more detailed self-assessment is possible.

### Invent your own marking scheme

Encourage your learners to devise their own marking schemes for self-assessment and to discuss which symbols would be appropriate for their use.

### Activity: Marking an essay

Learners can practise using their marking schemes by correcting Sabine's essay. They could also try correcting one another's work, either in a group or individually. The more discussion there is between learners, the more familiar with and confident about this type of self-assessment they should become.

## 2 Test yourself in a practice activity

When the class have read Javier's suggestions for testing himself, reinforce the point that text reconstruction exercises are very helpful for testing yourself. When taking notes from the model text, learners should only be concerned with the content, especially the main ideas, so that when reconstructing the text they are testing themselves on the appropriate textual features.

Elicit other ideas for testing yourself and discuss these with the class. Encourage the learners to test themselves regularly.

### 3   Assess your peformance in a real-life situation

It is clear from Mazharuddin's comments that he has disciplined himself
to assess his written work even in situations where little time is available.
Note that since Mazharuddin's practice examinations are not specifically
designed for improving his written English, but are to help him pass his
final examinations in medicine, we consider this an example of a real-life
situation.

### 4   Examples

In order to give your learners an example of how to use the self-
assessment chart, ask them to look at those filled in by Javier and
Mazharuddin. Encourage your learners to keep records of their progress.

──────   ■ ■ ■ ■ □ □ □   ──────

# Step 4   What do you need to do next?

| | |
|---|---|
| Materials: | Learner's Book page 100 |
| Items to cover: | Examples of learners' short-term aims. |
| Time: | 15–20 minutes when you introduce setting short-term aims in this skill for the first time. Thereafter, 5–10 minute sessions when necessary. |

If you are doing a Step 4 for the first time, read pages 67–8 in *2.1 Extending vocabulary*. If your learners are doing a Step 4 for the first time, refer
them to page 32 in *2.1 Extending vocabulary* in the Learner's Book. They
should then look at the examples of how Javier and Mazharuddin set
themselves short-term aims.

■■■■■□□

# Step 5   How do you prefer to practise your writing?

| | |
|---|---|
| Materials: | Learner's Book pages 101–104 |
| Items to cover: | 1. *Personal strategies* |
| | 2. *Time to experiment* |
| | Writing drafts |
| | Activity: Class guide |
| | Activity: Create a magazine |
| | 3. *Suggestions* |
| | Model Banks |
| | Memorise |
| | 4. *Choose a new strategy* |
| Time: | 45 minutes |

## 1   Personal strategies

Ernst, Marie Jesus, Luang and Martine use a variety of strategies for practising writing both for communication purposes and for personal reasons. Check that the class understand the strategies described. Elicit from your learners what they do and encourage an exchange of information.

If your institution has word-processing facilities for the learners, do not neglect these as an aid to developing writing skills, or as a way for learners to keep records of their written work and progress on disc. For further details see Piper (1987).

## 2   Time to experiment

### Writing drafts

The aim here is to encourage learners to think in English and to discourage them from translating. Ask learners to think about some of the disadvantages of translation: for example, it can lead to a very stilted style and there are some things that can't be translated. Encourage your class to write directly in English by writing drafts; this should help them become aware of how much they already know and reduce unnecessary dependence on dictionaries.

*Activity: Class guide*

Direct the learners to the instructions in their books. When comparing the drafts in class, look for good points as well as mistakes; this will reinforce the point that a draft is only a rough version and is not expected to be perfect.

*Activity: Create a magazine*

Creating a class magazine can be a useful way of motivating learners to draft and produce writing of different kinds. It is a good idea for learners to see examples of the types of writing they will be doing and for them to have sufficient time to draft, correct and rewrite their own texts before they are 'published' in the magazine. Different types of writing could include:

| | |
|---|---|
| letters | interviews |
| stories/poems | puzzles/games |
| recipes | editorials |
| reports | advertisements |
| articles | reviews |
| descriptions (e.g. fashions) | |

Learners can choose their own areas of interest to concentrate on and work at their own pace. In our experience, it is necessary to set aside a regular class or period of time for working on such a project.

## 3   Suggestions

*Model Banks*

Encourage your learners to keep scrapbooks or files of the types of writing they are interested in. In this way learners create personalised reference books suited to their own needs. This may require self-discipline and take time initially, but in the long run it will save effort and increase confidence and independence.

*Memorise*

Remind learners that learning certain phrases or expressions by heart can be very helpful. Ask them to make a list of expressions they think they will need to use regularly, such as formulaic phrases in writing formal letters, and to learn them.

## 4   Choose a new strategy

Encourage your learners to experiment with new strategies for practising their writing in order to help them find the one(s) they prefer.

■ ■ ■ ■ ■ □

# Step 6   Do you need to build up your confidence?

| | |
|---|---|
| Materials: | Learner's Book page 105 |
| Items to cover: | *Writing spontaneously*<br>Activity: Dictation<br>Activity: Timed writing |
| Time: | Build in short sessions as desired. |

### Writing spontaneously

Ask your learners to read the introduction to Step 6 in their books.

These activities aim to help learners build up their confidence, as well as to train them to think in English and write spontaneously without worrying about making mistakes. Encourage your learners to use dictionaries for checking *after*, not during, their work.

### Activity: Dictation

Dictate a part of a text to your learners and then ask them to continue writing the text on their own, developing the topic further and using the same style. Ask them to read their texts to each other in pairs or to the class.

### Activity: Timed writing

a)  Five minutes
    Give the learners a topic to write about; choose easy topics to begin with, like breakfast, houses, holidays, etc. Although they must write as much as they can, the text should be legible and make sense!
b)  Two minutes
    Again, choose easy topics to begin with. Encourage your learners to write as as much as they can without worrying about mistakes.

    You will probably find it helpful to repeat this activity on a regular basis.

■ ■ ■ ■ ■ ■

# Step 7   How do you organise your writing practice?

| | |
|---|---|
| Materials: | Learner's Book page 106 |
| Items to cover: | Suggestions. |
| Time: | 10 minutes |

Ask your learners to look at the suggestions in the Learner's Book for organising their writing practice and encourage an exchange of ideas.

---

**Further reading**

Allwright, J. forthcoming. This paper describes how reformulation was used as a feedback strategy in writing classes for non-native speakers of English studying at Lancaster University.
Byrne, D. 1979. A practical handbook which evaluates controlled and guided composition exercises and shows how to build them into a writing programme. Special attention is paid to the communicative purpose of writing activities.
Freedman, A. et al. 1983. Selected papers from the 1979 Canadian Council of Teachers of English – Learning to Write. These give an account of current research and practice into the product and process of writing, the place of writing in the cognitive development of young learners, points for the design of writing tasks and classroom practice.
Fried-Booth, D.L. 1986. A handbook for teachers containing a variety of activities to introduce students gradually to project work. It covers the organisation of a project, the monitoring of a project in action, and guidelines on how to develop and integrate the four skills. It also includes descriptions of case studies, and an appendix to build up useful addresses for resources.
Hedge, T. 1988. A discussion of the components of writing ability shown by skilled writers and how classroom activities can help learners to develop these. The first part of the book focusses on 'authoring' skills: developing a sense of audience, planning, drafting, and revising. The second section considers elements of 'crafting': the way in which a writer puts together the pieces of the text and chooses correct and appropriate language. It presents a range of writing tasks with the emphasis on the process involved in producing complete, contextualised pieces of writing.
Jolly, D. 1984. This covers a wide range of text-types which a student may need to write in English. Authentic examples of each type of text are followed by a number of practice writing tasks. The Teacher's Book can also be used as a self-study guide.

Pincas, A. 1982. Guidelines for planning writing courses and a discussion of the specific skills required: logical organisation of ideas, linking devices, emotive tone, formulating, etc. There are also a variety of writing exercises from controlled to free writing.

Piper, A. 1987. This paper argues that the word processor has the capacity to engage learners more closely in the activity of writing and can motivate them to write more by referring to two intermediate learners studying in London in a multilingual EFL class where English is the only common language.

Smith, F. 1982. An analysis of what writing involves for a writer and for a child learning to write. Smith explores interaction between the writer and the text and the reader/writer contract.

White, R. 1980. A practical guide to the teaching of writing set in the context of the functional use of language for communication. It examines what communicating in writing involves and gives detailed procedures for teaching different types of writing.

*Recommended for learners*

Coe, N. et al. 1983. This book aims to develop students' writing ability at upper-intermediate and more advanced levels through problem-solving activities.

Hedge, T. 1985a. A four-part supplementary series which encourages students to express their ideas in clear, concise, and correct English, and teaches techniques and strategies relevant to the planning and organisation of writing tasks. The levels range from elementary to intermediate.

Lewis, M. 1983. 22 suggestions for project work inside and outside the classroom which give students an opportunity to use their English for real communication.

You may find it useful to photocopy the Lesson Planning Sheet on the facing page and to produce your own version of the accompanying chart on page 24; there is no need to write to Cambridge University Press for permission.

LESSON PLANNING SHEET

Date: ...............................................

Class: ..............................................

Length of lesson: ...................................

Materials: ..........................................

....................................................

....................................................

<u>Objectives</u>

| | |
|---|---|
| Structural | |
| Functional | |
| Skills | |
| Phonological | |
| Lexical | |
| Learner training | |
| Anticipated difficulties | |

Evaluation: ........................................

....................................................

....................................................

# Bibliography

Aitchison, J. 1983. *The Articulate Mammal*. (2nd edn.) London. Hutchison.
   1987. *Words in the Mind*. Oxford. Basil Blackwell.
Alatis, J.E. 1976. 'The Urge to Communicate vs. Resistance to Learning in English as a Second Language', *ELTJ*, Vol. 30, 4:265–81.
Allwright, J. forthcoming. 'Don't correct – reformulate!', *Academic Writing: Process and Product*. ELT Documents 129. London, Modern English Publications in association with the British Council.
Allwright, R.L. 1977. 'Motivation – The Teacher's Responsibility?', *ELTJ*, Vol. 31, 4:267–73.
   1982. 'Perceiving and pursuing learners' needs' in *Individualisation*. Geddes, M. and Sturtridge, G. (eds.) London. Modern English Publications.
Altman, H.B. and James, C. V. (eds.) 1980. *Foreign Language Teaching: Meeting Individual Needs*. Oxford. Pergamon.
Baker, A. 1981. *Ship or Sheep?* Cambridge University Press.
   1982a. *Tree or Three?* Cambridge University Press.
   1982b. *Introducing English Pronunciation*. Cambridge University Press.
Bell, J., Boardman, R. and Buckby, T. 1985. *Variety*. Cambridge University Press.
Bialystok, E. 1985. 'The compatability of teaching and learning strategies', *Applied Linguistics*, Vol. 6, 3:255–62.
Blissett, C. and Hallgarten, K. 1985. *A very simple grammar of English*. Hove. Language Teaching Publications.
Blundell, L. and Stokes, J. 1981. *Task Listening*. Cambridge University Press.
Bolitho, R. and Tomlinson, B. 1980. *Discover English*. London. Allen and Unwin.
Bradford, B. 1988. *Intonation in Context*. Cambridge University Press.
Brazil, D., Coulthard, M. and Johns, C. 1980. *Discourse Intonation and Language Teaching*. Harlow. Longman.
British Council. 1978. *Individualisation in Language Learning*. ELT Documents 103. London. British Council.
British Council and Macmillan 1984. *Video English*. London. Macmillan.
Brown, G. and Yule, G. 1983. *Teaching the Spoken Language*. Cambridge University Press.
Bruce, K. and Ellis, G. 1987. 'Promoting equal opportunities in the foreign language classroom', *TESOL France News*, Vol. VII, 3:19.
Burstall, C. 1975. 'Factors affecting foreign language learning: a consideration of some recent research findings', *Language Teaching and Linguistics Abstracts*, Vol. 8, 1:5–25.
Buzan, T. 1982. *Use Your Head*. (Revised edn.) London. Aerial Books/BBC.
Byrne, D. 1979. *Teaching Writing Skills*. Harlow. Longman.
Carroll, J.B. 1967. 'Research problems concerning the teaching of foreign or second languages to younger children' in H.H. Stern, *Foreign Languages in Primary Education*, pp.94–109. Oxford University Press.
Carter, R. 1987. 'Vocabulary and second/foreign language teaching', *Language Teaching*, Jan. pp.3–16.

Chalker, S. 1984. *Current English Grammar*. London. Macmillan.

Channell, J. 1981. 'Applying semantic theory to vocabulary teaching', *ELTJ*, Vol. 35, 2:115–22.

Close, R.A. 1981. *English as a Foreign Language*. (3rd edn.) London. Allen and Unwin.

Coe, N., Rycroft, R. and Ernest, P. 1983. *Writing Skills*. Cambridge University Press.

Crookall, D. 1983. 'Learner training: a neglected strategy – Parts 1 and 2', *Modern English Teacher*, Vol. 11, 1 and 2: 41–2, 31–3.

1985. 'Read round a theme with a Ladybird: Parts 1 and 2', *Modern English Teacher*, Vol. 12, 3 and 4: 21–6, 40–3.

Davies, E. and Whitney, N. 1979. *Reasons for Reading*. London. Heinemann.

1981. *Strategies for Reading*. London. Heinemann.

1984. *Study Skills for Reading*. London. Heinemann.

Dickinson, L. 1981. 'Self-access materials', *Language Training*, Vol.2, 1:7–8.

1987. *Self-instruction in Language Learning*. Cambridge University Press.

Dickinson, L. and Carver, D. 1980. 'Learning how to learn: steps towards self-direction in foreign language learning in schools', *ELTJ*, Vol.35, 1:1–7.

Dulay, H., Burt, M. and Krashen, S. 1982. *Language Two*. Oxford University Press.

Dutra, I. 1985. 'Hypothesis-testing and problem-solving software for ESL students'. Paper presented at the 19th Annual Convention of TESOL, New York, 8–14 April 1985.

Eastwood, J. and Mackin, R. 1982. *A Basic English Grammar*. Oxford University Press.

Ellis, G. and Sinclair, B. 1986a. 'A systematic programme of learner training: train the learner to learn more effectively', in S. Holden (ed.) *Techniques of Teaching from Theory to Practice*, pp. 71–7. London. Modern English Publications in association with the British Council.

1986b. 'Learner training: a systematic approach', *IATEFL Newsletter*, 92:13–14.

1987. 'Teacher training for learner training?', *IATEFL Newsletter*, 96:29–30.

forthcoming. 'Helping learners discover their learning styles', Acts of the European Seminar on Learning Styles, CRAPEL, Université de Nancy II, 26–29 April 1987.

Elsworth, S. 1982. *Count Me In*. Harlow. Longman.

Ely, P. 1985. *Bring the Lab back to life*. Oxford. Pergamon.

Entwistle, N.J. and Ramsden, P. 1983. *Understanding Student Learning*. Beckenham. Croom Helm.

Faerch, C. and Kasper, G. 1983. *Strategies in Interlanguage Communication*. Harlow. Longman.

Ferris, D. 1983. 'The influence of the continuous self-evaluation of oral skills on language learning methodology', in *Contributions to a renewal of language learning and teaching – Some current work in Europe*, pp. 171–7. Strasbourg. Council of Europe.

Fitzpatrick, A. 1987. *English for International Conferences*. Englewood Cliffs, N.J. Prentice-Hall.

Flinders, S. 1984. 'Language learning profiles and the French Grande Ecole student', *Language Training*, Vol. 5, 4.

Freedman, A., Pringle, I. and Yalden, J. (eds.) 1983. *Learning to Write: First Language / Second Language*. Harlow. Longman.

Freire, P. 1972. *Pedagogy of the Oppressed*. Harmondsworth. Penguin.

Fried-Booth, D.L. 1986. *Project Work*. Oxford University Press.

Fröhlich, M. and Paribakht, T. 1984. 'Can we teach our students how to learn?', in P. Allen and M. Swain (eds.) *Language Issues and Education Policies*. ELT Documents 119. London. British Council.

Gairns, R. and Redman, S. 1986. *Working with Words*. Cambridge University Press.

Gardner, R.C. and Lambert, W.E. 1972. *Attitudes and motivation in second language learning*. Rowley, Mass. Newbury House.

Geddes, M. and Sturtridge, G. (eds.) 1982. *Individualisation*. London. Modern English Publications.

Gomes de Matos, F. 1986. 'A gap in ESL pedagogy: learners' rights', *TESOL Newsletter*, Vol. XX, 2:9.

Grandcolas, B. 1986. 'Un journal d'apprentissage pour préparer à l'enseignement', *TESOL France News*, Vol. 6, 3:16–20.

Grandcolas, B. and Soulé-Susbielles, N. 1986. 'The analysis of the foreign language classroom'. *Studies in Second Language Acquisition*, Vol. 8: 293–308.

Grellet, F. 1981. *Developing Reading Skills*. Cambridge University Press.

Hallgarten, K. and Rostworowska, B. 1985. (Pilot edn.) *Learning for Autonomy – Learner Training Materials for ESL and Literacy Groups in Adult Education*. London. ALBSU, Independent Learning Project.

Harding-Esch, E. (ed.) 1976. *Self-Directed Learning and Autonomy*. Report of a seminar held at the University of Cambridge, 13–15 December 1976. University of Cambridge, Department of Linguistics and CRAPEL (mimeo).

Harding-Esch, E. 1982. 'The open access sound and video library of the University of Cambridge: progress report and development', *System*, Vol. 10, 1:13–28.

Hassall, S. 1983. 'An application of "The Good Language Learner" to EFL learners in Bahrain', *TESOL France News*, Vol. 4, 1:15–22.

Hawkins, E. 1984. *Awareness of Language: An Introduction*. Cambridge University Press.

Hedge, T. 1983a. *Pen to Paper*. Walton-on-Thames. Nelson.
    1983b. *In a Word*. Walton-on-Thames. Nelson.
    1985a. *In the Picture*. Walton-on-Thames. Nelson.
    1986. *Freestyle*. Walton-on-Thames. Nelson.
    1985b. *Using Readers in Language Teaching*. London. Macmillan.
    1988. *Writing*. Oxford University Press.

Higgs, D. 1985. 'Learners'. Training Manual *Teaching and Learning in Focus*. London. British Council.

Holden, S. 1983. *Focus on the Learner*. London. Modern English Publications.

Holec, H. 1981. *Autonomy and Foreign Language Learning*. Oxford. Pergamon.
    1988. (ed.) *Autonomy and self-directed learning: present fields of application*. Strasbourg. Council of Europe.

Hughes, A. and Trudgill, P. 1979. *English Accents and Dialects*. London. Edward Arnold.

Illich, I. 1973. *Deschooling Society*. Harmondsworth. Penguin.

James, P. 1985. 'Word Trees', *Modern English Teacher*, Vol. 12, 4:31–4.

Jolly, D. 1984. *Writing Tasks*. Cambridge University Press.

Jones, C. 1985. *Wordstore*. London. Wida Software.

Jones, L. 1981. *Functions of English*. Cambridge University Press.

Kolb, D.A. 1984. *Experiential Learning*. Englewood Cliffs, NJ. Prentice-Hall.

Krashen, S. 1981. *Second Language Acquisition and Second Language Learning*. Oxford. Pergamon.

Lewis, M. 1983. *Projects*. Hove. Language Teaching Publications.
    1986. *The English Verb*. Hove. Language Teaching Publications.

Lewkowicz, J.A. and Moon, J. 1985. 'Evaluation: a way of involving the learner', in *Lancaster Practical Papers in English Language Education*, Vol. 6: 45–80. J.C. Alderson (ed.).

Lindstromberg, S. 1985. 'Schemata for ordering the teaching and learning of vocabulary', *ELTJ*, Vol. 39, 4:235–43.

Littlejohn, A. 1985. 'Learner choice in language study', *ELTJ*, Vol. 39, 4:253–61.

Littlewood, W. 1984. *Foreign and Second Language Learning*. Cambridge University Press.

Marshall, L.A. and Rowland, F. 1983. *A Guide to Learning Independently*. Milton Keynes, Open University Press.

McConnell, J. 1981. 'Technicians and Language', *Language Training*, Vol. 2, 4.

McDowell, J. and Hart, C. 1987. *Listening Plus*, London. Edward Arnold.

Mortimer, C. 1985. *Elements of Pronunciation*. Cambridge University Press.

Murphy, R. 1985. *English Grammar in Use*. Cambridge University Press.

Naiman, N., Fröhlich, M., Stern, H.H. and Todesco, A. 1978. *The Good Language Learner*. Research in Education Series, 7. Ontario Institute for Studies in Education.

Narcy J.P. 1983. 'Les besoins d'apprentissage, stratégies d'apprentissage et de communication: Comment les évaluer?', *Echanges Pédagogiques*, 1:45–60.

Nisbet, J. and Shucksmith, J. 1986. *Learning Strategies*. London. Routledge & Kegan Paul.

Norrish, J. 1983. *Language learners and their Errors*. London. Macmillan.

Nuttall, C. 1982. *Teaching Reading Skills in a Foreign Language*. London. Heinemann.

Ockenden, M. 1983. *Small Talk*. Harlow. Longman.

O'Malley, J.M., Chamot, A.U., Stewner-Manzanares, G., Kupper, L. and Russo, R.P. 1985a. 'Learning strategies used by beginning and intermediate students', *Language Learning*, Vol. 35, 1:21–46.

1985b. 'Learning strategy applications with students of English as a second language', *TESOL Quarterly*, Vol. 19, 3:557–84.

Oskarsson, M. 1980. *Approaches to Self-assessment in Foreign Language Learning*. Oxford. Pergamon.

Oxford-Carpenter, R. 1985. 'Second language learning strategies: What the research has to say', *ERIC/CLL News Bulletin*, Vol. 9, 1.

Palmer, R. and Pope, C. 1984. *Brain Train*. London. E. and F.N. Spon.

Pincas, A. 1982. *Teaching English Writing*. London. Macmillan.

Piper, A. 1987. 'Helping learners to write: a role for the word processor', *ELTJ*, Vol. 41, 2:119–25.

Porter Ladousse, G. 1982. 'From needs to wants: motivation and the language learner', *System*, Vol. 10, 1:29–37.

Prowse, P. and McGrath, I. 1984. *Advances*. London. Heinemann.

Reiss, M.A. 1983. 'Helping the unsuccessful language learner', *Forum*, Vol. XXI, 2:2–7.

Richterich, R. and Chancerel, J.L. 1980. *Identifying the needs of adults learning a foreign language*. Oxford. Pergamon.

Riley, P. 1985. 'Strategy: conflict or collaboration?' *Mélanges Pédagogiques*: 91–116. CRAPEL, Université de Nancy II.

1986. 'Who's who in self-access', *TESOL France News*, Vol. 6, 2:23–34.

Rivers, W.M. 1983. *Communicating Naturally in a Second Language*. Cambridge University Press.

Rogers, C. 1969. *Freedom to Learn*. Colombus, Ohio. Merrill.

Rubin, J. 1975. 'What the "Good Language Learner" can teach us', *TESOL Quarterly*, Vol. 9, 1:41–51.

Rubin, J. and Thompson, I. 1982. *How to be a More Successful Language Learner*. Boston. Heinle & Heinle.

Rudzka, B., Channell, J., Putseys, Y. and Ostyn, P. 1981. *The Words You Need*. London. Macmillan.

1985. *More Words You Need*. London. Macmillan.

Scott, M., Carioni, L., Zanatta, M., Bayer, E and Quintanilha, T. 1984. 'Using a "standard exercise" in teaching reading comprehension', *ELTJ*, Vol. 38, 2:114–20.

Shepherd, J., Rossner, R. and Taylor, J. 1986. *Ways to Grammar*. London. Macmillan.

Sinclair, B. and Ellis, G. 1984. 'Autonomy begins in the classroom', *Modern English Teacher*, Vol. 11, 4:45–7.

Skehan, P. forthcoming. *Individual Differences in Second Language Learning*. London. Edward Arnold.

Smith, F. 1978. *Reading*. Cambridge University Press.

1982. *Writing and the Writer*. London. Heinemann.

St Clair Stokes, J. 1984. *Elementary Task Listening*. Cambridge University Press.

Stern, H.H. 1975. 'What can we learn from the good language learner?', *Canadian Modern Language Review*, Vol. 31: 304–18.

1983. *Fundamental concepts of Language Teaching*. Oxford University Press.

Stevick, E.W. 1976. *Memory, Meaning and Method*. Rowley, Mass. Newbury House.

1982. *Teaching and Learning Languages*. Cambridge University Press.

Swan, M. 1980. *Practical English Usage*. Oxford University Press.

Swan, M. and Smith, B. (eds.) 1987. *Learner English*. Cambridge University Press.

Toney, T. 1983. 'Guides for language learners', *ELTJ*, Vol. 37, 4:352–58.

Underhill, A. 1980. *Use Your Dictionary*. Oxford University Press.

Underhill, N. 1981. 'Your needs are different from my needs', *World Language English*, Vol. 1, 1:15–18.

Wallace, M.J. 1980. *Study Skills in English*, Cambridge University Press.

1982. *Teaching Vocabulary*. London. Heinemann.

Watcyn-Jones, P. 1985. *Test your Vocabulary*. Harmondsworth. Penguin.

Wenden, A.L. 1985a. 'Learner Strategies', *TESOL Newsletter*, Vol. XIX, 5.

1985b. 'Facilitating learning competence: perspectives on an expanded role for second-language teachers', *Canadian Modern Language Review*, Vol. 41, 6:981–90.

1986a. 'Helping language learners think about learning', *ELTJ*, Vol. 40, 1:3–12.

1986b. 'Incorporating learner training in the classroom', *System*, Vol. 14, 3:315–25.

Wenden, A.L. and Rubin, J. 1987. *Learner Strategies in Language Learning*. Englewood Cliffs, NJ. Prentice-Hall.

White, R. 1980, *Teaching Written English*. London. Heinemann.

Whitling, D. 1982. 'What sort of language learner are you?' *Business Express*, Vol. 3, 1.

Whitney, N. 1983. *Checkpoint English 1*. Oxford University Press.

1985. *Checkpoint English 2*. Oxford University Press.

Williams, R. 1982. *Panorama*. Harrow. Longman.

Windeatt, S. 1980. 'A project in self access learning for English language and study skills in *Lancaster Practical Papers in English Language Education*, Vol. 3:43-82.

# Typology of learning strategies in Learning to Learn English

Since the early 1970s research in language acquisition has focussed more closely on learner characteristics and their possible influence on the language learning process. Learning strategies give the learner the chance to make choices and exercise control, thereby possibly learning more effectively.

Rubin (1975:43) defines learning strategies as: 'techniques or devices which a learner may use to acquire knowledge.' A number of studies have now attempted to classify learning strategies in various ways. However, the data-elicitation techniques, the diverse range of learners and the different learning settings (naturalistic or classroom) used by the researchers in their studies have resulted in the use of varied and sometimes overlapping terminology. This has sometimes made it difficult to compare the strategies reported in one study with these in another. Consequently, as far as we are aware, a definitive typology of language learning strategies does not yet exist. However, outside the field of second language learning, many authors have emphasised the difference between those strategies which are more generalised (Metacognitive strategies) and those which are more task specific (Cognitive strategies). O'Malley et al. (1985a) applied this scheme to language learning and added a further category, which they called socioaffective. (See page 12 for further details.)

The following Typology covers the learning strategies included in the Learner's Book. They are listed under the categories of Metacognitive, Cognitive, Social and Communication and are based on descriptions provided by O'Malley et al. (op:cit) and studies described in Faerch and Kasper (1983), as well as in Riley (1985). We have extended these categories and adapted descriptions where necessary.

## Metacognitive

| Strategy | Description | Reference |
|---|---|---|
| Advance preparation | Planning and preparing oneself for a language activity. | 2.5, Step 5,2(c); 2.3, Step 6,1; 2.4, Step 6,2; 2.3, Step 7,3,4. |
| Analysing needs | Analysing linguistic needs or wants in order to clarify long-term aims. | 1.3,1. |
| Comparing | Analysing and comparing differing language items from L1 or L2. | 2.2, Step 2,1(a), 1(b), 2; 2.4, Step 2,1(c), 5(a), 5(c), 5(d); 2.6, Step 2,2,3; 2.6, Step 3,2. |
| Directing attention | Deciding in advance to attend to a specific language item(s) and ignore distractors. | 2.2, Step 5,1; 2.5, Step 5,1. |
| Discussing | Reflecting on, sharing ideas about and experiences of language learning. | 1.1, 1,2; 1.5, (b); 1.6, 1,3; 2.1–2.6, Step 1,3; 2.4, Step 3,1,2,3; 2.1, Step 5, 1(d), 2(b), 2(c). |
| Expanding subject awareness | Finding out about English and language learning. | 2.1, Step 2,1,2; 2.2, Step 2,1,2; 2.3, Step 2,1; 2.4, Step 2, 1–5; 2.5, Step 2,1; 2.6, Step 2,1,2,3. |
| Expressing beliefs | Reflecting on attitudes and beliefs about language learning. | 1.1,(b); 2.1–2.6, Step 1,1,2; 2.2, Step 3,1(b). |

| Strategy | Description | Reference |
|---|---|---|
| Expressing preferences | Reflecting on preferred learning strategies. | 2.1–2.6, Step 5. |
| General self-assessment | Assessing one's general language proficiency. | 1.1,(a); 1.2; 1.3,2. |
| Joining a study group or club | Meeting with other learners to learn or practise collaboratively outside class. | 2.4, Step 5,1; 2.2, Step 7,6; 2,3 Step 7,6; 2.4, Step 7,4; 2.5, Step 7,4. |
| Keeping a diary | Writing a personal record of and reflecting on language learning, daily events and experiences. | 2.6, Step 5,1. |
| Negotiating | Discussing and reaching agreement with other learners and teachers. | 1.1, (c); 1.3,2. |
| Prioritising | Prioritising learning according to one's personal needs and/or wants. | 1.3,2; 2.1, Step 2,2. |
| Resourcing | Finding out about and maximising the potential of available resources for learning inside and outside the classroom including the use of L2 reference materials. | 1.4, 1,2,3; 1.6,2; 2.1–2.4, Step 3,2,3; 2.2–2.6, Step 5,1; 2.1–2.6, Step 7. |
| Reviewing | Systematic revision in order to aid long-term retention. | 1.4,6; 2.2, Step 7,3. |
| Selecting criteria | Identifying appropriate criteria for self-assessment, pre- or post-performance. | 2.1–2.6, Step 3. |
| Self-management | Understanding the conditions that help one learn and arranging for the presence of these conditions. | 1.1(c); 1.4,4,5; 1.5,(a); 1.6,5; 2.6, Step 3; 2.3, Step 5; 2.5, Step 5; 2.6, Step 5, 2.1–2.6 Step 7. |
| Self-reward | Rewarding oneself when a language learning activity has been accomplished successfully. | 2.1, Step 3,2. |
| Setting short-term aims | Selecting what to work on next and how to do it, based on self-assessment and priorities. | 2.1–2.6, Step 4. |
| Specific self-assessment | Checking one's performance for accuracy, fluency and appropriacy against self-selected criteria either during or after an activity. | 2.1–2.6, Step 3,2,3. |
| Strategy evaluation | Assessing the effectiveness and relevance of a specific learning strategy. | 1.6,3(c), 3(d), 4(b); 2.5, Step 2,2; 2.1, Step 5,1(c), 1(d), 4; 2.2, Step 5,3; 2.3, Step 5,3; 2.4, Step 5,2(c), 3; 2.5, Step 5,3; 2.6, Step 5,4; 2.1, Step 6; 2.5, Step 6,2. |

## Cognitive

| Strategy | Description | Reference |
|---|---|---|
| Audio-recording | Recording oneself for the purpose of self-assessment. | 2.2, Step 3,3; 2.3, Step 3,3; 2.4, Step 3,1,2,3; 2.4, Step 5,1,2; 2.4, Step 6,1. |
| Auditory | Listening to language models several times in order to aid comprehension and retention. | 2.1, Step 7,1; 2.3, Step 5,1. |

| Strategy | Description | Reference |
|---|---|---|
| Collecting | Building up resource banks of specific language examples. | 2.2, Step 5, 2(a); 2.2, Step 7,5; 2.3, Step 7,2,4; 2.5, Step 7,2; 2.6, Step 7,3,4. |
| Contextualisation | Placing a word or phrase in a meaningful language sequence. | 2.1, Step 3,2; 2.1, Step 7. |
| Copying | Copying a text in order to practise writing. | 2.6, Step 7,5. |
| Defining | Using L2 to clarify meaning and aid retention. | 2.1, Step 3,2. |
| Directed physical response | Relating new information to physical actions. | 2.5, Step 3. |
| Drafting | Preparing to write a final version of a text. | 2.6, Step 5,2. |
| Experimenting | Trying out different learning strategies. | 1.6,3; 2.1, Step 5; 2.1, Step 6,(a)–(d), 2.2, Step 2,2; 2.2, Step 5,3; 2.2, Step 6; 2.3, Step 5,3; 2.3, Step 6,1,2; 2.4, Step 5,3; 2.5, Step 5,3; 2.5 Step 6,2; 2.6, Step 5,2,3,4. |
| Grouping | Reordering or reclassifying (perhaps relabelling) the material to be learned based on common attributes. | 2.1, Step 5,1,2; 2.1, Step 7. |
| Imagery | Relating new information to visual concepts in the memory using familiar, easily retrievable visualisations or phrases. | 2.1, Step 5,3. |
| Inferencing | Using available information to guess the meanings of new items, predict outcomes, fill in missing information and understand grammar rules. | 2.2, Step 5; 2.2, Step 6; 2.3, Step 2,1; 2.5, Step 6,2. |
| Keeping a diary | (See Metacognitive.) | |
| Listening for gist | Listening to find out the general meaning. | 2.3, Step 2,1,2; 2.3, Step 5,1. |
| Memorising | Learning language items by heart. | 2.6, Step 5,3. |
| Noting down | Writing down important items as they occur. | 2.1, Step 7; 2.6, Step 3,2. |
| Oral repetition | Imitating a language model to aid retention and production. | 2.1, Step 5,1. |
| Predicting | Using clues from the context to guess possible content. | 2.3, Step 6,2; 2.5, Step 6,1,2. |
| Reading aloud | Reading aloud from a text in order to practise pronunciation, stress, rhythm, etc. | 2.4, Step 7,6. |
| Reading for detail | Reading a text very carefully. | 2.5, Step 2, 2(c). |
| Reconstructing | Rebuilding a text from a set of notes. | 2.6, Step 5,1. |
| Risk taking | Feeling confident enough to try something out in L2 and not worrying about making mistakes. | 2.1, Step 6; 2.2, Step 6; 2.3, Step 6,2; 2.4, Step 6,1,2; 2.5, Step 6,1,2; 2.6, Step 6. |
| Role-playing | Acting out situations either alone or with other learners. | 2.4, Step 5,1. |
| Scanning | Looking quickly for a specific point in a written text. | 2.5, Step 2, 2(b). |
| Selecting and rejecting | Listening for specific information and ignoring irrelevant detail. | 2.3, Step 2,2. |
| Skimming | Reading a text quickly just to understand the main ideas. | 2.5, Step 2, 2(a). |

# Typology of learning strategies

| Strategy | Description | Reference |
|----------|-------------|-----------|
| Summarising | Producing a summary of an oral or written text to check comprehension. | 2.5, Step 3,2. |
| Translation | Using L1 as a base for understanding and/or producing L2. | 2.1, Step 3,2; 2.1, Step 5,1. |
| Visual reinforcement | Using visual stimuli to clarify meaning and aid retention. | 2.1, Step 3,2; 2.1, Step 5,1; 2.1, Step 7. |
| Word building | Using one's linguistic knowledge of L2 (or another language) to derive words from or understand a particular form. | 2.1, Step 7; 2.5, Step 6,2. |
| Written repetition | Imitating a language model several times in order to aid retention and production. | 2.1, Step 5,1; 2.1, Step 7. |

## Social

| Strategy | Description | Reference |
|----------|-------------|-----------|
| Discussing | (See Metacognitive.) | |
| Joining a study group or club | (See Metacognitive.) | |
| Negotiating | (See Metacognitive.) | |
| Resourcing | (See Metacognitive.) | |
| Role-playing | (See Cognitive.) | |

## Communication

| Strategy | Description | Reference |
|----------|-------------|-----------|
| Appeals | Asking a speaker to speak more slowly, clearly, etc. | 2.3, Step 5,2. |
| Approximation | Using an incorrect L2 word to convey the meaning, since it shares essential semantic features with the target word. | 2.1, Step 6,(iv). |
| Checks | Checking and confirming that the meaning of a message has been understood, e.g. by repeating information, reformulating or summarising. | 2.3, Step 5,1. |
| Creating time to think | Using 'Thinking-time' techniques when speaking in order to sound fluent and provide time to make an appropriate response. | 2.4, Step 6,1. |
| Foreignising | Using a borrowed word or phrase from L1 and giving it an L2 pronunciation. | 2.1, Step 6,(i). |
| Paraphrasing | Describing some aspect of an item, e.g. appearances, function. | 2.1, Step 6, (ii),(iii). |
| Word coinage | Inventing a new word based on knowledge of either L1 or L2. | 2.1, Step 6,(v). |
| 'Wossernaming' | The use of substitute words with no meaning to fill gaps in the speaker's vocabulary. | 2.1, Step 6,(vi). |

154